Great Walks of Yosemite National Park

Text by Robert Gillmore
Photographs by Eileen Oktavec

To Joseph Paul Oktavec, 1911-1993, artist, writer and connoisseur, whose love and keen interest in our work is cherished.

Great Walks ®

No. 5 in a series of full-color, pocket-size guides to the best walks in the world published by Great Walks Inc. Guides already published: *Great Walks of Acadia National Park & Mount Desert Island, Great Walks of Southern Arizona, Great Walks of Big Bend National Park, Great Walks of Sequoia & Kings Canyon National Parks* and *Great Walks of the Great Smokies.* For more information on all Great Walks guides send $1 (deductible from your first order) to: Great Walks, PO Box 410, Goffstown, NH 03045.

Copyright © 1993, © 1996 by Great Walks Inc. Library of Congress Catalog Card Number: 93-77158
ISBN: 1-879741-05-9

*COVER: The magnificent monolith **Half Dome** seen from the Sentinel Bridge over the Merced River in Yosemite Valley.*

CONTENTS

Acknowledgments

We are grateful for the assistance of Dean Shenk of the National Park Service, Jim Nett of the Yosemite Association and Ann Fraser and Keith Walklet of Yosemite Concessions Services Corporation.

What Are Great Walks?

Great Walks invariably offer beautiful and interesting world-class scenery and excellent views in the most picturesque places on earth.

Great Walks are also shorter and easier than the typical hike or climb. They're usually less than five miles long. They can always be walked in a day or less.* And they're almost always on smooth, firm, dry and, most important, *gently graded* trails. (Long, arduous, sweaty treks up rough, steep, rocky trails are *not* Great Walks!)

* One exception: Three-day back-country excursions where you spend your nights and take your meals at three different High Sierra Camps.

What Are
Great Walks Guides?

Great Walks guides carefully describe and, with beautiful full-color photographs, lavishly illustrate the world's Great Walks.

Unlike many walking guides, which describe *every* trail in a region, Great Walks guides describe only the *best* walks, the happy few that will especially delight you with their beauty.

Unlike many guides, which give you mainly directions, Great Walks guides carefully describe *all* the major features of every Great Walk so you can know, in advance, precisely what the Walk has to offer and *why* it's worth your time to take it.

After all, your leisure time is valuable. In your lifetime you can walk only a fraction of the hundreds of thousands of miles of trails in the world. Why not walk only the best?

For your convenience Great Walks guides are an easy-to-use and easy-to-carry pocket size and our covers are film laminated for extra protection against wear and tear.

Introduction:
The Wonders of
Yosemite — And
How to Enjoy Them

When John Muir called Yosemite "the incomparable valley" he was being uncharacteristically restrained: He was praising only the seven-mile-long valley at the base of Half Dome. But Yosemite is more than an incomparable *valley;* it's an incomparable *park.* For no other park has so many natural wonders in just one place. Yosemite Valley, for example, is not only a world-famous gallery of natural rock sculpture: *Over* these half-mile-high granite promontories flow some of the highest waterfalls in the world and the tallest cataract in North America. These features help make the valley the gem of the park. But the park as a whole boasts enough natural treasures to make Yosemite the crown jewel of *all* the national parks. Besides major waterfalls and awesome bare rock domes *outside* Yosemite Valley, the park has beautiful rockbound lakes, flower-filled meadows, two-mile-high Sierra Nevada peaks that are snowcapped even in summer, and vast groves of giant sequoia trees, the world's largest living things, whose trunks are as wide as rooms.

You can see all these natural wonders on some or all of 28 Great Walks. Walks No. 1-3, 5-13, 16 and 26 all offer views of major waterfalls. Walks No. 4,

16, 18, 19, 21-25, 27 and 28 take you along the shores of beautiful lakes. Walk No. 5 is a stroll along the cascading Merced River. Walks No. 8-13 provide stunning views of Yosemite Valley and nearby landmarks from overlooks on or near the valley's south rim. Walks No. 14 and 15 take you through groves of giant sequoias. Walks No. 17-19 and 27 offer views of the domes and other rock sculpture in the Tenaya Lake basin. Walks No. 20-22 and 26 show you Tuolumne Meadows and the domes and mountains around it. Walks No. 23-28 feature views of the snowcapped peaks of the Sierra Crest.

None of these Walks is strenuous. In fact, 11 of them — Nos. 1-5, 8, 15, 17, 18, 20 and 25 — are easy or very easy. Four others — Nos. 10, 11, 14 and 24 — while not quite easy, are nevertheless undemanding. All the others are moderate, except for Nos. 23 and 27, which are moderately strenuous.

Virtually all the Walks are easily reached on well-paved, two-lane roads that take you to scenery that often rivals that seen on the Walks. Also, all the Walks are at or near accommodations that are satisfactory at worst and splendid at best. (See *How to Get There, Where to Eat, Where to Stay*, below.)

What's the best time to take these Walks? Right after the snow melts. That's when the trails are clear, the waterfalls and cascades (most of which are made of melting snow) are fullest and early wildflowers are blooming. For Walks No. 1-16 the best time is usually after mid-May and before mid-June — when, incidentally, you get another bonus: the park is less crowded than it gets in the summer. The best time for the high-country Walks — Nos. 17-25 — is usually after mid-June and before the snow and cold return in September.

Walks No. 26-28, of course, can't be taken before the High Sierra Camps open in July or after they close in early September. Also, Nos. 6-15 and 17-28 — all but six of the Walks — can't be taken from October to May because some or all of the trails are covered with snow and/or because the roads to the trailheads are closed because of snow. (Some Walks, of course, can be skied or snowshoed in the winter. Check with park rangers for more information about this alternative.) See *How to Get There, Where to Eat, Where to Stay,* below.

Many waterfalls in Yosemite, including those in Yosemite Valley, are snow fed, so they're reduced to a trickle and may even disappear entirely by late summer. Also, Mirror Lake (Walk No. 4) dries up by late summer. These water features are at their best in either late spring or early summer at the latest.

What are the very *best* Walks, the ones to take if you have time for just a few? Walks No. 1, 3 and 8 — Yosemite Falls, Bridalveil Fall and Glacier Point — are three very short, easy strolls that will show you the best of the valley, Yosemite's *creme de la creme.* If you have time, add No. 6, the Mist Trail to Vernal Fall; No. 14 or 15, the Mariposa and Tuolumne groves of giant sequoias; and Nos. 17 and 20, Olmsted Point and Tuolumne Meadows, two quick and easy Walks along the Tioga Road. If you can spend several days in the park, skip Walk No. 6 and do No. 7, Nevada Fall, which includes No. 6; also do No. 9, Sentinel Dome; No. 16, Wapama Falls; No.

21, Lembert Dome & Dog Lake; and No. 23, the Gaylor Lakes—all longer and more demanding than our first choices.

In all, it takes about ten days to do the first 25 Walks— particularly if you take time to enjoy the scenery (see below)—and another nine days to do Nos. 26-28, the High Sierra Camps.

How long does each Walk take? That depends, of course, on how fast you walk, how often and how long you stop, etc. But a handy rule of thumb is: one hour per mile.

Here is some more information as well as a few suggestions to help you get the most out of these Great Walks:

▶Read the entire guide, or as much of it as you can, before taking any of the Walks. That way you'll be familiar with the Walks before you take them and you can select the Walks that most closely suit your taste.

▶Carry the guide on all the Walks. (It'll fit easily in any pocket.) It gives you exact directions for each Walk, including how to get to the trailhead, as well as detailed descriptions of what you'll see.

▶Follow our directions. The Walks start where they start, stop where they stop and go where they go for two reasons: (1) the routes we describe provide the best walking in Yosemite; (2) other trails are more difficult, less scenic or both.

▶Nearly all trailheads and trail junctions are well marked, almost every trail is easy to follow and we tell you everything you need to know to find your way. If, however, you like to follow a map or want to use one to help identify the park's natural landmarks, we recommend the handsome and informative *Map & Guide to Yosemite Valley* and the *Map & Guide to Wawona and the Mariposa Grove of Big Trees,* both published by Rufus Graphics, as well as a topographic map of the entire park and one of the Tuolumne Meadows area, both published by Wilderness Press. All four maps are available, for modest prices, at visitor centers and stores throughout the park.

▶Two publications you might want to buy are the detailed *Yosemite Road Guide,* which explains what all those numbered posts along the park roads mean (it's especially useful for pointing out what you see from the many viewpoints in Yosemite Valley), and *Wildflowers of Yosemite,* whose precise descriptions and color photographs identify the park's many blooming plants.

▶Three handy publications are available without charge. The park's *Official Map and Guide* clearly and attractively indicates all roads in and around the park, as well as major trails, creeks, mountains and other natural and manmade features. The *Yosemite Guide,* published by the Yosemite Association, gives dates and times of park activities. Both are distributed at park entrance stations and visitor centers. The colorful *Yosemite Magazine,* which describes the park's many tourist amenities, is available from the park concessioner, Yosemite Concessions Services Corporation (see *How to Get There, Where To Stay, Where to Eat,* below).

▶Unless you're in excellent condition (and few people are) do your body a favor: Do as many of the Walks as possible in order of difficulty, easy ones first. That way each Walk you take will make it easier for you to do the more difficult Walk that follows. Ideally you'll be able gradually to get in shape for the more difficult Walks, such as Nos. 23 and 26-28.

►Walking in high altitudes (above 8,000 feet) is easier after you've taken a day or so to get accustomed to the thinner air. That's another reason for doing the easier Walks along the Tioga Road (Nos. 17, 18, 20, 24 and 25) before the harder ones—and certainly before setting off to the High Sierra Camps.

►Any comfortable walking shoes are fine for short Walks that follow smooth paths (Nos. 1-5, 8, 15, 20 and 25, for example). For other Walks we recommend the greater support and protection provided by above-the-ankle hiking boots. To avoid unnecessary discomfort (or even blisters) make sure your footwear fits and is broken in.

►Many park trails—particularly those on longer Walks—are used by horses and mules. To avoid startling them when they pass, move off the trail and stand still.

►Don't worry about black bears. Unlike grizzlies (which don't live in California), black bears don't attack people unless they think they're threatening their cubs. So if you see a bear, keep your distance, look for cubs (they may be in a tree) and make sure you don't come between them and their mother.

►Don't feed *any* wild animals. Human food isn't good for them. If bears become accustomed to human food, and to the places where it's found, they become nuisances (by breaking into cars, etc.) and have to be destroyed. Conclusion: If you really want to be nice to animals, admire them but let them find their own dinner. And make sure you leave food and food wastes where bears and other wild animals can't get them. All your garbage should be put in refuse containers.

►Ordinarily, summer weather in the Sierra is excellent for walking. It's fair and comfortable and rain is rare. (Most of the precipitation in the park is winter snow.) But it does rain occasionally. To stay dry (and avoid possible hypothermia) we suggest you carry rain gear and wear waterproof hiking boots on cloudy days and especially on longer Walks. For best protection, we recommend a water-proof hooded jacket and pants. The most comfort-able rain garments are "breathable," which means they keep rain out but also let perspiration escape.

►Remember that the weather gets cooler as the altitude gets higher. If your excursion involves a big change in elevation, bring along a sweater, jacket or windbreaker.

►Carry water on longer Walks. It will taste best if you carry it in ceramic canteens, such as the French-made Tournus, rather than plastic or metal bottles. If you have access to a refrigerator, here's a way to keep it cold: The night before a Walk pour a couple of inches of water in the canteen and lay the canteen on its side in the freezer, leaving the top open to make sure the canteen doesn't crack when the water freezes and expands. Next morning fill it up with cold water. The ice already inside the canteen will keep the water cold.

►Never drink water from any stream or spring in

the park without either boiling it, filtering it or treating it with purifying tablets. The risk of an attack of *giardia lamblia* is too great to drink un-treated water.

►Don't urinate or defecate within 50 feet of creeks or lakes and don't wash yourself or your dishes in them. (Even biodegradable soap should not be used in lakes or streams; all soaps pollute.)

►Begin each Walk early enough to complete it comfortably before dark.

►On longer Walks, carry a small flashlight in case you can't get back before dark, as well as some toilet paper and Band-Aids.

►It's obvious but it bears repeating: Binoculars let you see what you can't see without them. A high-powered, light-weight pair is worth carrying.

►The closer you get to the sun in the high, thin mountain air the more powerful are its rays. Use enough sun screen to protect the exposed part of your body and use something to keep the sun out of your eyes. We favor a wide-brimmed hat or a sun visor over tinted sunglasses, which substitute a tinted view of the world for the real one. Also, a hat or visor helps keep you cool by protecting much of your face from the sun.

►Climbing up waterfalls or down cliffs is danger-ous. The National Park Service warns you not to do it, and so do we. Also, be sure to walk only on established trails.

►We carefully describe the falls, cascades and other water features you'll see on these Walks. Keep in mind, however, that they may look different in unusually wet or dry weather and, as noted above, many will diminish and even disappear in late summer or fall.

►Remember that the world's only constant is change. The locations of the mountains on these Walks won't vary from year to year. But anything subject to human control—trail routes, parking lots, signs and so on—can change. Be alert for trail reroutings and follow signs.

►Above all, remember that a Great Walk is mainly an aesthetic activity, not an athletic one. Its primary purpose is not to give you exercise (although exercise you will certainly get) but to show you exceptional natural beauty. Walk slowly enough to savor it. Most people, in fact, walk too fast. Don't make their mistake. You no more want to rush through these Walks than you want to rush through the Louvre.

How to Get There, Where to Stay, Where to Eat

Nearly half the Walks — Nos. 1-13 — begin in or near Yosemite Valley, which is entered from the west (and only from the west) by three roads.

* * *

Route 140, also known as the Merced Road, comes into the park at El Portal and follows the Merced River upstream into the valley. As you approach Yosemite Valley you'll enjoy frequent views of the cascading Merced, on your right.

About two miles east of El Portal you'll go through the Arch Rock Entrance Station and then drive under Arch Rock, two enormous boulders leaning against each other, after which the station is named.

In another three miles you'll reach the bridge over the Cascades, which are formed where Tamarack and Cascade creeks come together just south of Route 120 (see below). Leave your car in a parking area before the bridge, walk across the concrete span, then watch the 500-foot cascades splashing down the steep granite walls of the Merced canyon.

In another 1.7 miles you'll reach the intersection of Route 120. About a mile after that you'll come to Pohono Bridge, where the valley loop road begins.

* * *

Unlike Route 140, Routes 41 and 120 approach the valley not from below but from above it. They therefore offer (among other things) memorable high-level views of both the valley and the Merced canyon.

* * *

Route 120 becomes the Big Oak Flat Road at the park's Big Oak Flat Entrance and then passes spring-blooming dogwoods and giant firs, pines and other evergreens.

About 15 miles from the park entrance the road descends through an area that was scarred by a forest fire in 1990.

In another mile you'll come to a parking area on the right, where you'll have a stunning view of Yosemite Valley. El Capitan is on the left, Sentinel Dome (Walk No. 9) is on the right and Half Dome is an impressive focal point in the middle. You can also see Elephant Rock and Turtleback Dome on the steep south wall of the Merced River canyon.

Then the road runs through a half-mile-long tunnel and, immediately after it, brings you to an even more impressive view of Yosemite Valley. Ahead of and below you is an enormous evergreen-festooned gouge in the earth, 3,000 feet deep and a mile wide. But the valley isn't just big. From here it's also a powerful composition. Its linear focal point is two long ribbons of water: the thin, white Bridalveil Fall (Walk No. 3) on the gray granite wall of the valley and, below the falls, the sparkling Merced River. On both sides of the fall, creases in the rock walls point to the cascade and emphasize its central-ity. On either side of both the river and the fall, the nearly vertical gray walls of the flat-bottomed valley sweep thousands of feet upward.

Immediately after this viewpoint the road crosses Tamarack and Cascade creeks. Leave your car in a parking area on the right, walk out on the bridges and watch the creeks tumbling over granite rocks up- and downstream. The dark green incense ce-dars and other evergreens contrast beautifully with the gray rock and white water.

The road now clings to nearly vertical rock walls as it descends to the valley. In two places the walls are so steep that the road can't remain *on* them but must go *through* them in tunnels. Over the handsome fieldstone walls on the right side of the road you'll have dramatic views of the narrow, steep-sided Merced canyon.

Finally the Big Oak Flat Road runs into Route

140 on the banks of the Merced, at the bottom of the valley.

* * *

Route 41, also known as the Wawona Road, comes into the park at its southern entrance near Wawona. Like Route 120, the road passes two stirring overlooks of Yosemite Valley.

After its intersection with the Glacier Point Road, the highway gradually descends into the valley. Along the way you'll have views of the steep walls of the Merced River canyon on your left.

About six miles after the Glacier Point Road intersection, at a parking area on the left, you'll have your first view of Yosemite Valley. You'll see El Capitan on the north side of the valley, on your left; Half Dome, in the eastern end of the valley; and, from left to right, Sentinel Rock, Sentinel Dome and Cathedral Rocks, on the south side of the valley.

Then the road passes through the .8-mile Wawona Tunnel, the longest of four tunnels in the park. Immediately after the tunnel, in a parking area on the left, you'll have another view of Yosemite Valley. Here you'll see El Capitan, Half Dome and the flat, forested valley floor plus Bridalveil Fall rushing down the south wall of the valley.

You'll catch glimpses of the fall as the road keeps descending to the valley loop road, which is about 1.5 miles from the tunnel.

* * *

You can drive to three of the Yosemite Valley's Great Walks—Nos. 1-3—on the loop road. To get to the others—Nos. 4-7—you'll have to walk, bicycle (on a paved road) or ride the free Shuttle Bus, which stops at all campgrounds, hotels and other services in the valley and runs every day, all day and early evening. Its route and schedule are published in the *Yosemite Guide*.

Yosemite Valley offers many kinds of accommodations.

Lodging spans the spectrum from campgrounds to cabins (with or without baths) to motor lodges to the grand Ahwahnee Hotel, where the cheapest room costs more than $200 a night in the summer. The only housekeeping accommodations, however, are tents with gas stoves but no refrigerators. If you want a motel room with a kitchenette, you have to go to El Portal. If you'd prefer a condominium, there are some fine ones for rent in Yosemite West, a community just to the west of the park and, like El Portal, about ten miles from Yosemite Valley. The Park Service has a complete list of lodgings outside the park. To get a copy call 209-372-0200 or write to Yosemite National Park, PO Box 577, Yosemite, CA 95389. The park concessioner, Yosemite Concessions Services Corporation, can provide more information about accommodations *in* the park. Call 209-252-4848 or write to the company at 5410 East Home, Fresno, CA 93727.

Food services in the valley include snack bars, food stores (one of them large), a delicatessen, two cafeterias and several restaurants, including the Ahwahnee's magnificent dining room, perhaps the grandest in any national park. Dinner at the Ahwahnee requires reservations — sometimes weeks in advance — and costs about twice as much as in any other restaurant in the area. Breakfast or lunch, however, is an underrated pleasure: The dining room is seldom crowded during the day (unlike other restaurants in the valley), reservations are not necessary, the food is always the best for miles around, and breakfast and lunch cost only a couple of dollars or so more than at restaurants nearby. The Ahwahnee is a serene, beautiful oasis in an often bustling valley. It's a delight to slip away from the crowds and enjoy the quiet sumptuousness of the most beautiful building in the park.

* * *

Walks No. 8-13 all begin at or near Glacier Point, on the rim of Yosemite Valley. Glacier Point is at the eastern end of the Glacier Point Road, which, because of snow, is closed beyond the Badger Pass Ski Area from October to May.

To get to Glacier Point from Yosemite Valley, head south on Route 41 (the Wawona Road) and, about 10 miles from the valley loop road, take a left onto the 16-mile-long Glacier Point Road.

In a couple of miles you'll have views of the Merced canyon, more than 4,000 feet below, on your left.

Six miles from Route 41 you'll pass the lush Summit Meadow, on your right, where large drifts of wildflowers bloom beside patches of snow as late as June.

In another 1.5 miles you'll suddenly have a view, straight ahead, of 11,726-foot Merced Peak, one of the summits of the Clark Range. It's flecked with snow even in summer. Three and a half miles farther along you'll see the entire Clark Range on your right. The sharp-pointed, bare-rock peaks include, from left to right, 11,522-foot Mount Clark, 11,573-foot Gray Peak, 11,699-foot Red Peak and Merced Peak. Left of Mount Clark is the smooth, rounded granite of 9,092-foot Mount Starr King.

In another 2.5 miles you see the bare rock of 8,122-foot Sentinel Dome (Walk No. 9), just to the left of the road, and a few hundred feet ahead you pass the trailhead for Walk No. 9 and No. 10 (Taft Point).

Soon the road starts switching sharply back and forth as it descends to the rim of Yosemite Valley. In another mile it comes to Washburn Point, whose 180-degree vista of bare rock sculpture rivals that from Glacier Point. Turn into the parking area and enjoy the view. The panorama includes, from left to right, North and Basket domes, on the north rim of Yosemite Valley, Tenaya Canyon, Half Dome, Mount Broderick, Liberty Cap, Nevada Fall (Walk No. 7) and the Emerald Pool behind it, Vernal Fall (Walk No. 6), the milky-white scribble of the Merced River, Panorama Cliff, Mount Clark, Mount Starr Ring and other peaks of the Clark Range. You'll also hear Illilouette Fall and you may even be able to glimpse the top of the fall below Mount Starr King. This view is worth a long look and there are picnic tables here if you want to eat while you enjoy the scenery.

The road keeps switching back and forth until, less than a mile from Washburn Point, it reaches Glacier Point (Walk No. 8). A snack bar here serves hot dogs, sandwiches and beverages, as well as ice cream, cookies and other snacks; so if you like, you can put together a pretty good lunch before or after a Walk.

HOW TO GET THERE, WHERE TO STAY . . . 21

You can drive to Glacier Point if you're taking Walks No. 8 and 11. For Walks 12 and 13—both one-way trips to the bottom of Yosemite Valley—you'll probably have to get a ride or, more likely, take the tour bus. The comfortable, air-conditioned coach leaves Yosemite Lodge in Yosemite Valley at 8:30 A.M. and, since it makes only one stop, it arrives at Glacier Point by 10 A.M. The driver will point out points of interest on the way and describe how Yosemite Valley was created by glaciers. To make sure you get a seat, make a reservation at the Tour Desk in the lodge on the day before your trip. You can make the reservation in person or you can call (209) 372-1240.

* * *

Walk No. 14, the Mariposa Grove of giant sequoias, is near the southern entrance of the park and seven miles from Wawona, the second largest community in the park (after Yosemite Village, in the valley). Located in this village is the Pioneer Yosemite History Center, an interesting collection of relocated 19th century buildings; two grocery stores; dozens of housekeeping cabins; and the handsome, 19th-century Wawona Hotel. The restored hotel, a big, white, wooden landmark, is the oldest accommodation in the park. Its amenities include a nine-hole golf course, a swimming pool and a popular dining room, walled on two sides with enormous windows, that serves tasty breakfasts, lunches and dinners. (In the winter the Wawona is closed on weekdays and the road to the Mariposa Grove may be closed because of snow.)

* * *

Walk No. 15, the Tuolumne Grove of giant sequoias, begins about .5 miles north of the junction of the Big Oak Flat Road and the Tioga Road in Crane Flat. There's a grocery store and gas station at the junction, which is about 8.5 miles east of the park's Big Oak Flat Entrance and about 10 miles from the intersection of the Big Oak Flat Road and Route 140, near the entrance to Yosemite Valley.

* * *

Walk No. 16, Wapama Falls, is at the Hetch Hetchy Reservoir, about seven miles northeast of the park's Hetch Hetchy Entrance and about 35 miles from the intersection of the Big Oak Flat Road and Route 140. The only services between Yosemite Valley and the trailhead are the grocery store and gas station in Crane Flat; a snack bar at Camp Mather, which is about .5 miles south of the Hetch Hetchy Entrance; and the Evergreen Lodge, a woodsy resort .5 miles south of Camp Mather that has cabins (without baths), a restaurant and a grocery store-snack bar.

* * *

Walks No. 17-28 all begin on or near the eastern half of the Tioga Road, which runs across the middle of the park from the Big Oak Flat Road, at its western end, to the Tioga Pass Entrance, at its eastern end. The Tioga Road is closed from October to May because of snow.

If you're approaching the Tioga Road from Yosemite Valley, take the Big Oak Flat Road (Route

HOW TO GET THERE, WHERE TO STAY ... 23

120) to Crane Flat; then turn right onto the Tioga Road.

About .5 miles north of the Big Oak Flat Road, you'll pass the Old Big Oak Flat Road, on your left, on which you walk to the Tuolumne Grove of giant sequoias (Walk No. 15). Then the Tioga Road climbs through an evergreen forest and, about 7.5 miles from the Big Oak Flat Road, crosses the South Fork of the Tuolumne River. In spring and early summer 50-foot cascades tumble over the ledges on the south side of the bridge.

In another 6.2 miles you'll pass the pretty, one-acre Siesta Lake on your right and a mile later you'll come to the road to White Wolf Campground. The dining room there serves breakfast and dinner in the summer (reservations are recommended for dinner) and a small store sells groceries and snacks.

Two miles after the White Wolf Campground turnoff you have a view of the Clark Range and 10,850-foot Mount Hoffmann, which is in the center of the park. You're now in more open, more rocky terrain and you start to see snowcapped peaks through the evergreens. You'll also have views into the canyon of Yosemite Creek, the source of Yosemite Falls (Walks No. 1-2).

About three miles after your view of Mount Hoffmann and the Clark Range, you'll cross Yosemite Creek, which cascades over ledges on your left.

About 4.5 miles farther, on the right, is an interesting exhibit on the evergreen trees you'll see on the Walks in this area. Plaques explain the characteristics of three types of pine and two kinds of fir.

You also have a view of Clouds Rest, Half Dome and the Clark Range.

In another 2.5 miles you'll see Half Dome again and 9,092-foot Mount Starr King to the right of it. Two miles later you'll see Mount Starr King again and the wide, flat slope of Clouds Rest to its left.

The best view on the Tioga Road, however, is another 1.5 miles ahead, at Olmsted Point (Walk No. 17). Here you'll see not only Clouds Rest and Half Dome but also the rock basin of Tenaya Lake (Walk No. 18), which is about 1.5 miles beyond Olmsted Point.

Five miles after Lake Tenaya is Tuolumne Meadows, the largest subalpine meadow in the Sierra Nevada. Walks No. 17-28 all begin either in the meadows or within 11 miles of them.

Unlike all the other Great Walks in Yosemite, Walks No. 17-28 all begin more than 50 miles from Yosemite Valley. So instead of staying in the valley, we recommend that, to be as close to Walks 17-28 as possible, you stay in either the campground in Tuolumne Meadows; a tent cabin at Tuolumne Lodge, just east of Tuolumne Meadows; or in a motel room or housekeeping cabin at the rustic Tioga Pass Resort, in the Inyo National Forest, about two miles north of the park's Tioga Pass Entrance. All these accommodations are popular and require reservations well in advance of your stay. Campground reservations are made through Destinet at 1-800-436-7275. Reservations at the Tuolumne Lodge are made by calling 209-252-4848. The Tioga Pass Resort can be reached at 209-372-4471 or 619-376-3945. If you can't get into the

Tioga Pass Resort or any accommodation in the park, there are several motels in Lee Vining, a small town about 11 miles east of the park.

Food services in the area include a grocery store and a snack bar in Tuolumne Meadows; a restaurant serving breakfast and dinner (reservations recommended for dinner) at Tuolumne Lodge; a cafe and small grocery store at the Tioga Pass Resort; motels, restaurants and a large grocery store in Lee Vining; and some fine restaurants in Mammoth Lakes, a spiffy resort about 25 miles south of Lee Vining.

* * *

The last three Walks, Nos. 26-28, are all three-day excursions on which you eat your meals and spend your nights at High Sierra Camps. The camps are rustic resorts in the wilderness. You sleep in concrete-floored tent cabins furnished with steel bunks, wood stoves (nights are cool in the High Sierra), wood shelves and folding tables and chairs. The comfortable beds are made up with mattresses, three blankets, a comforter and a pillow. A towel, washcloth, soap and candles are provided.

A few tents have only two beds but most have four and a few have six or eight, which means you'll probably share your tent with strangers. But that's seldom, if ever, a problem: Most people we've met at these (and other) backcountry camps are pleasant at worst and very companionable at best. In fact, we've made many friends at these places.

Breakfast and dinner are served family style in a dining tent. The food is tasty and portions are generous. One memorable dinner was tomato soup, green salad, filet mignon (medium rare), pasta with light cream and garlic sauce, eggplant parmesan and chocolate chip cookies. Breakfast is usually fruit juice, scrambled eggs, bacon, pancakes and muffins or biscuits. Coffee, tea and hot chocolate are served with all meals. Box lunches are also available (for an additional charge) and usually include fresh fruit, raisins, nuts, some kind of pastry and a big sandwich (choices range from peanut butter to corn beef). Lemonade or hot chocolate, depending on the weather, is served during the day. A small camp store sells candy, drugs and other sundries.

All you need to bring are what you would bring on any long day hike (including a flashlight), plus personal toilet articles, changes of socks and other clothes, something warm to sleep in and bed linen. (The Yosemite Concession Services Corporation, which operates the camps, sells a handy one-piece, 13-ounce cotton-and-polyester "travel sheet.")

Unfortunately most camps accommodate only 30 to 50 guests and the demand for reservations vastly exceeds the supply. Accommodations are therefore assigned by lottery. Literally thousands of people apply for reservations in the fall, the lucky few are selected in the winter and the results are announced in the spring. However, if you arrive in Yosemite without reservations—or without all the reservations you'd like—don't despair. Cancellations are common. Just call the High Sierra Desk at 209-454-2002 and inquire about openings. You might get lucky.

And if you can get only one night's reservation instead of two, you can turn a three-day excursion into a two-day trip simply by walking only the first and third day's itinerary.

Great Walks of Yosemite

1 Yosemite Falls

This easy half-mile round trip offers close, continuous views of the world's second highest waterfall, which drops a total of 2,425 feet down the granite walls of Yosemite Valley.

Like many other valley falls Yosemite is fed mainly by melting snow, so it's fullest in spring but starts drying up in summer and often disappears completely by fall. Try to see it as early in the season as you can.

The eight-foot-wide asphalt trail to the base of the falls begins just .5 miles west of Yosemite Village and just north of Yosemite Lodge on the Yosemite Valley loop road. The trailhead parking area is on the north side of the road. (Restrooms with flush toilets are under the trees on the northwest side of the parking area.)

The trail to the falls begins, on the north side of the parking area, as a dramatic, 400-foot-long, arrow-straight *allee* lined with tall evergreens pointing directly at Upper and Lower Yosemite Falls. The *allee* is stunning for two reasons: first, because it's a formal design that you expect to find in an 18th-century French garden, not in a park, where virtually every path is an endless, irregular curve; second, because the *allee* tightly frames both sides of the falls and fixes the eye firmly on the long, narrow white ribbon of water ahead of you.

As you walk down the *allee,* past giant, three-foot-thick ponderosa pines, go slowly and contemplate the complexity of the largest waterfall in North America. The upper fall pours through a notch on the top of the sheer granite wall of the valley, then drops 1,430 feet — more than a quarter of a mile — to the crags below. Buffeted by breezes on its long journey downward, the fall spreads wider and thins out. Much of the water seems to turn into air. Sometimes the fall seems to fall slowly, gently, like white gauze or white smoke. Sometimes the wind is so strong that the upper fall sways to the right or left, like the pendulum of a clock. John Muir said he once saw the entire fall stop in mid-air, "resting on the invisible arm of the North Wind," and that it stayed there while he counted to 190! But don't be fooled by appearances. The airiness of the upper fall is an illusion, as Muir himself discovered one night when he was caught underneath the fall. So much water, falling from so great a height, was like hailstones crashing into his body, Muir reported.

The base of the upper fall is hidden by the ever-green-festooned crags of the Middle Cascades. There, out of sight, Yosemite Falls drops another 675 feet in a series of rapids, cascades and pools before pouring out of the rock as the lower fall, which plunges another 320 feet into Yosemite Valley.

Partly because the lower fall drops less than a

quarter of the distance of the upper fall, it has less exposure to the effects of the wind and doesn't break up like the upper fall. On the contrary, while the upper fall is thin, wispy and slightly gray, the lower fall is thick, turgid and milk white.

Though only the smallest of the three Yosemite Falls, the lower fall is almost twice as high as Niagara and it's thrilling enough to make this walk a Great Walk all by itself. And when all three Yosemite Falls are combined in a nearly half-mile-high vista of falling water the effect is unparalleled.

At the end of the *allee,* below the falls, the trail curves to the right, winds gently upward through oaks and cabin-size boulders and emerges at a paved observation point and a footbridge over Yosemite Creek, about 50 feet below the base of the lower fall. From here you can see and hear the fall crashing loudly into the rocky creek bed. So hard does the enormous column of water hit the rocks that it springs up and away from them in an unending series of water explosions. The blasts turn the fall into a fine mist that enshrouds the bottom of the cataract and can often be felt by onlookers more than 60 feet away.

If you walk out onto the bridge and look downstream you'll see small cascades in the cold, pellucid water of 50-foot-wide Yosemite Creek. Further south, you'll see the towering, bare gray eminence of 7,038-foot Sentinel Rock on the south wall of Yosemite Valley.

When you're ready, follow the walkway back to the parking lot. When you get back to the *allee* turn around and enjoy the view of Yosemite Falls again.

2 Yosemite Falls Vista

This easy 1.5-mile ramble through Yosemite Valley's most scenic meadow is the only Great Walk in the middle of the valley's nearly level floor. It offers continuous views of a dozen Yosemite landmarks, including Yosemite Falls (Walk No. 1), North Dome, the Royal Arches, Half Dome, Sentinel Rock, Cathedral Spires and Cathedral Rocks.

The Walk begins at the Yosemite Falls Viewpoint, on the southern, west-to-east section of the one-way Yosemite Valley loop road, about 500 feet west of the Yosemite Chapel. To get to the trailhead by car you'll have to approach it from the west. Parking is along the left (north) side of the road. You'll see Yosemite Falls on your left before you get out of your car.

You're now in the middle of a broad, grassy meadow bisected by the loop road and surrounded by the valley's nearly vertical half-mile-high granite walls. As you walk across the meadow toward the falls on one of two boardwalks (take either one) you'll get better and better views of Yosemite's world-famous natural features, all of which are part of the valley's walls. Ahead of you, on the north wall of the valley, is Upper Yosemite Fall, which flows through a notch on top of a sheer gray cliff and gradually becomes wider, thinner and airier as it falls, seemingly leisurely, almost a quarter of a mile down the valley walls. It seems that if the fall had to fall even farther it would literally disappear into thin air. To the right of the fall is Yosemite Point and, below it, the hard-to-see natural obelisk known as the Lost Arrow. Further to the right, and much easier to see, are the giant concentric half-circles in the valley wall known as the Royal Arches. Above the arches, on top of the valley wall, is the smooth, rounded bare rock of 7,542-foot North Dome. Immediately to the right of the arches is the flat-faced rock tower called the Washington Column. To the right of the dome is Tenaya Canyon and to the right of the canyon, at the east end of the valley, is the highest point in the valley wall, the massive, flat-fronted, rounded 8,842-foot monolith known as Half Dome. Less than a mile behind you, looming over the south wall of the valley, is 7,038-foot Sentinel Rock. To your left, about three miles away, are the jagged Cathedral Spires and Cathedral Rocks.

The meadow will also give you a sense of what makes Yosemite Valley such a satisfying natural composition. The valley is a long outdoor room, or gallery, and its beauty lies in the extreme contrast between its vertical rock walls and its horizontal meadow-and-forest floor. The granite walls are gray, smooth and hard—the very essence of indestructi-

The 2,425-foot-high **Yosemite Falls**, *the tallest in North America and the second highest in the world, framed by evergreens on either side of the* allee *on Walk No. 1.* ▶

ble, inorganic permanence. The floor is the very opposite: green, rich-textured, soft and, like all organic things, perishable and impermanent.

The boardwalks end at the tree-shaded banks of the Merced River, which here is a smooth, 50-foot-wide stream meandering softly across the valley floor. Take the path to the right, which follows the edge of the Merced for about a quarter-mile before it comes to a handsome stone-and-wood footbridge over the river. The bridge is an excellent viewpoint from which to gaze down on the smooth bottom of the river through its utterly transparent water.

When you're ready to return to your car, retrace your steps to the road.

3 Bridalveil Fall

This gentle 1.5-mile round trip offers views of both 620-foot Bridalveil Fall—the most entertaining falling water in the park—and 1,612-foot Ribbon Fall, the third highest single fall of water in the world. The Walk also features vistas of the 7,569-foot monolith El Capitan and bird's-eye views of the Merced River.

The Walk begins at the Bridalveil Fall parking area, just south of the intersection of the Yosemite Valley loop road and the road to Wawona. If you're driving to the trailhead from the eastern end of the valley, you'll have to drive west on the one-way loop road to the Pohono Bridge over the Merced, then go east. In about .5 miles you'll turn right onto the Wawona Road and, in less than 300 feet, you'll take a left into the Bridalveil parking area (which, incidentally, has picnic tables, chemical toilets and a public telephone).

Look toward the eastern end of the parking area and you'll see Bridalveil Fall, less than a quarter-mile away, even before you get out of your car. The view is stunning in its verticality. The 200-yard-long white ribbon of water falls down, down, down the high, bare cliff and is framed on both sides by tall oaks and cedars that appear to reach almost as high as the waterfall. You can hear the water crashing on the boulders beneath it.

The wide, paved 1,000-foot walkway to the base of the fall begins at the eastern end of the parking lot. A sign warns you to be "prepared for heavy spray" and to "watch your footing on the wet pathway." If you plan to watch the fall for a while — and we suggest you do — you may want to bring along a rain jacket and a plastic bag for your camera, for in the spring and early summer the fall will bathe you in mist.

The walkway splits in about 150 feet. Go right and follow the path as it climbs gently along the east bank of noisily cascading Bridalveil Creek. The creek begins at Ostrander Lake, ten miles to the south and 4,500 feet above the valley. Then it flows north to Yosemite Valley, leaps over the rock wall of the valley as Bridalveil Fall and runs into the Merced a quarter-mile from the fall.

The path ascends to a paved viewpoint that's barely a couple of hundred feet from the fall. The often-misty vantage point is furnished with an enormous U-shaped bench made of logs more than two feet thick.

The fall begins as a tight, white column of water pouring horizontally — not vertically — over the top of the rock wall of the Valley. In fact, sometimes the wind on the fall is so strong that the water doesn't simply fall over the wall but, pushed by the wind, actually *rises* slightly, in apparent defiance of gravity, before descending gracefully into the valley. Sometimes the wind turns the column of water into smoky white mist, so it looks more like dry ice than water.

Like Upper Yosemite Fall, Bridalveil breaks up on its long journey downward. Sometimes it turns into long, graceful swags of water that descend leisurely down the cliff. Sometimes it becomes long, pointed, white shooting stars of water — which John Muir called "comets." Sometimes these water comets plunge all the way to the bottom of the fall; sometimes they dissolve into air, like meteors burning out in space.

Rarely does Bridalveil fall straight down. Often, in a temporary victory of wind over gravity, the entire fall is blown to one side like a veil in the wind. When the fall is blown to the right, it splashes over rocks below it and decorates them with dozens of

Yosemite Falls flowing over the half-mile-high walls of Yosemite Valley, as seen from **Yosemite Falls Vista** *(Walk No. 2).* ▶

little cascades.

So close is the fall, and so much and so intriguingly does the wind change its moods, that one simply cannot "see" it in a moment. Bridalveil demands lingering.

When, at last, you're ready to leave you have a choice. If you're short of time, you can follow the path back to your car. If, instead, you'd like to see a view of El Capitan and Ribbon Fall, follow the walkway back to the last trail junction and, instead of heading left toward the parking lot, go right and follow the old paved road through the woods. You'll quickly cross three branches of Bridalveil Creek on three handsome fieldstone bridges. Upstream you'll have another view of Bridalveil and the small, right-leaning rock peak, appropriately called the Leaning Tower, to the right of it.

The road soon becomes dirt as it curves to the left and heads toward the valley loop road. Very soon you'll see El Capitan ahead of you. About 100 feet from the loop road you'll see a trail on your right. A wooden sign says the path leads to Curry Village and the stables. Follow the smooth path upward through oaks and evergreens and across large talus slopes. Soon you'll be near the base of the smooth, almost vertical wall of the 6,000-foot Cathedral Rocks, on your right. You'll have to stretch your neck to see to the top of them. Below, on your left, the Merced surges over its rocky bed. Across the valley is El Capitan and, to the left of this monolith, the ultrathin and well-named Ribbon Fall, which descends in a single uninterrupted fall almost a third of a mile down the Yosemite Valley wall. Only the

Angel and Cuquenan falls in Venezuela have longer drops. Like Yosemite Falls, Ribbon Fall flows fully only in the spring and early summer. By midsummer it's just a trickle and by fall it usually disappears completely.

When the trail starts to descend into the woods, about a quarter of a mile from the last trail junction, turn around, retrace your steps to the parking area and enjoy the views again.

4 Mirror Lake

This two-mile round trip takes you easily into Tenaya Canyon, away from the cars of Yosemite Valley, and offers close views of Mount Watkins and Half Dome and photogenic reflections of both promontories in aptly named Mirror Lake.

Mirror Lake dries up by late summer so try to see it as early in the season as possible.

The trail to the lake is actually a paved road that's open just to bicyclists and walkers. It begins at Shuttle Bus Stop No. 17, about a quarter-mile east of the stables at the east end of the valley. The road to the trailhead is closed to cars, which are allowed no closer than the stables. You can walk to the trailhead or you can take a bicycle or the Shuttle Bus. (See pages 18-19 for more information on the bus.)

The walkway to the lake is level at first as it runs through a pleasant evergreen forest.

In less than .2 miles the trail crosses a handsome stone bridge over Tenaya Creek and in about .5 miles it starts climbing gently to the left of the cascading, rock-choked stream.

After about a mile the route passes a 30-foot-long wooden footbridge over the creek, then a large, placid pool with a small, sandy beach. Immediately after the beach the road reaches the west shore of tiny Mirror Lake. A plaque here explains that Mirror is a "disappearing lake," slowly filling up with silt transported by Tenaya Creek, and that this process is a "small-scale version of what happened in Yosemite Valley," when ancient, glacier-carved Lake Yosemite also filled up with water-borne sediments and the lake gradually became a marsh, then a meadow, then finally the fields and forests spread across the floor of Yosemite Valley today.

Follow the stone steps down to the lake and walk out to the tip of the 10-by-30-foot peninsula that juts into the lake from the north shore. On the west side of this little point is a charming, placid 20-by-40-foot pool rimmed by boulders. On the east side is the rest of the half-acre lake. Beyond the lake—where the lake *used* to be—is a low, grassy meadow. Beyond the meadow is the notch of Tenaya Canyon. To the left of the notch, the steep, bare rock slopes of 8,500-foot Mount Watkins rise a mile above the lake. To the right of the notch the nearly vertical face

Mule deer graze in the lush grass on the nearly level floor of Yosemite Valley. **Yosemite Falls** *(Walks No. 1 and 2) is in the background.* ▶

of Half Dome sweeps skyward. This scene creates a beautiful reflection in Mirror Lake and the best time to see it is in early morning, before the wind begins to ruffle the water, when few if any people are around and the only sounds you hear are the muffled flow of Tenaya Creek and the twittering of birds.

Mirror Lake is an idyllic picnic spot. It offers a quiet refuge from the bustle of the valley and the closest views of Half Dome from anywhere below it. The shores of Mirror Lake also provide views of 7,542-foot North Dome, 7,214-foot Glacier Point (Walk No. 8) and 9,926-foot Clouds Rest. In order to preserve this fragile area, however, the Park Service asks you to walk only on established trails.

When you're ready to return to Yosemite Valley, you can follow the paved road you walked in on or, if you'd like a change of scenery, you can follow the path through the woods on the south side of Tenaya Creek. The trail has good views of the cascading stream and fewer people than you'll meet on the road. (Unfortunately, the path is also a well-used horse trail; so if you want to avoid droppings, stick to the road.) You can pick up the trail on the south side of the footbridge over Tenaya Creek and follow it downstream, past boulders (many of them huge) and through pleasant woods. The path parallels the road, which is on your right, on the north side of the creek. It reaches the valley loop road about 60 feet east of Shuttle Bus Stop No. 17, where you began the Walk.

5 Happy Isles

This easy mile-long stroll is as pleasant as its name suggests. It takes you to twin islands in the Merced River and briefly down the river's east bank for continuing views of the torrent as it surges out of Merced Canyon. You'll also see Yosemite Falls, Illilouette Creek and Glacier Point and you can tour the Happy Isles Nature Center.

Like the Mirror Lake trail (Walk No. 4), the walk to Happy Isles begins on the eastern end of the Yosemite Valley loop road, which is closed to cars. The closest you can drive to the trailhead is the Day Use Parking area, about .7 miles to the west. From there you can bicycle or walk to the trailhead (a footpath runs along the south side of the loop road) or ride the free Shuttle Bus from Stop No. 14 at the Day Use Parking area to Stop No. 16 at the Happy Isles trailhead. (See pages 18-19 for more information on the Shuttle Bus.)

When you reach the trailhead you'll see a restroom building ahead of you and you'll hear (but not yet see) the Merced churning loudly on your left. You'll also see two wide, flat trails, one on each side of the restrooms, leading through the open woods. Each path runs parallel to the Merced and in less than .2 miles will take you to Happy Isles.

Follow the trail farther from the river and you'll

come first to the Happy Isles Nature Center, which has interesting re-creations of Yosemite's different natural environments, complete with stuffed birds and animals. Outside the building, near its entrance, is a large wall map of the site.

Follow the trail from the Nature Center to the handsome stout wooden bridge that takes you to the island closest to the west bank of the Merced. A sign here quotes W. E. Dennison, an early guardian, or superintendent, of the park, who said that he named the twin islets the Happy Isles because "no one can visit them without for the while forgetting the grinding strife of his world and being happy."

One is inclined to agree. But the attraction here isn't the islands per se—they're pleasant but unremarkable bits of open woods—it's the water raging all around them. The islands, and the bridges leading to them, are special not for what they are but for what they do: They take you into the middle of the Merced and provide long platforms from which to experience the river's frothy cascades.

To enjoy these water views to the fullest, take every path on the islands. Cross the bridge to the first island, follow the path upstream along the east side of the isle and retrace your steps downstream. Then cross the bridge from the first island to the second, follow the path upriver on the west side of the island, turn around and come back downriver. Next, cross the bridge from the second island to the

---

The 620-foot-high **Bridalveil Fall** *(Walk No. 3) makes rainbows as it crashes onto rocks in Yosemite Valley.* ▶

east bank of the Merced, where there are still more water views to come.

About 50 feet from the Merced you'll come to the John Muir Trail. Go left at the intersection and follow the path through a dark forest and past huge boulders. In a couple of hundred feet you'll come to another bridge over the Merced. You'll cross this bridge later. Right now keep walking downstream on the smooth, unpaved path on the right. (This is a popular bridle trail, so keep an eye out for droppings.)

The trail stays close to the river so you'll have constant views up and down the Merced. Very soon you'll pass under a stone arch bridge on which the loop road crosses the river and vistas will open up in almost all directions. Behind and above you is Illilouette Creek, flowing down Illilouette Canyon (Walk No. 12). To your left and more than 3,000 feet above you is Glacier Point (Walk No. 8). Ahead of you, to the left, is Upper Yosemite Fall (Walks No. 1 and 2). Directly ahead is the smooth, bare, rounded rock of 7,542-foot North Dome. These views last until the river, and the path beside it, start curving to the left about a third of a mile from Happy Isles.

Turn around here, go back upstream, cross the footbridge over the Merced that you passed earlier and enjoy more views of the churning river from the span.

After you cross the bridge you'll see a snack bar ahead of you that sells cold sandwiches, hotdogs, ice cream, yogurt, coffee, soda and other beverages. The banks of the Merced are terrific places to picnic.

When you're ready, follow the path heading west, away from the bridge. It curves to the right, follows the Merced downstream and ends at the trailhead, just to the right (east) of the restrooms.

6 Vernal Fall

This moderate three-mile round trip takes you to Vernal Fall on the well-named Mist Trail. You'll be exhilarated by the spray from the 317-foot fall and, below the fall, you'll have continuous views of rainbows. You'll also enjoy vistas of Yosemite and Illilouette falls, Panorama Cliff, Illilouette Ridge, Glacier Point and the roaring, rocky Merced.

This Walk is also part of the excursion to Nevada Fall (Walk No. 7) and the Panorama Trail (Walk No. 13), both much longer trips. If you plan to take either of those Walks, you may want to skip this one.

Like the trails to Happy Isles (Walk No. 5), this incomparable Walk begins at Shuttle Bus Stop No. 16, near the eastern end of the valley loop road. The closest you can drive to the trailhead is the Day Use Parking area, about .7 miles to the west. From there you can take the Shuttle Bus from Stop No. 14 to the trailhead. Or you can bicycle or walk on the foot-path running beside the loop road.

If you take this Walk in the spring or early summer, when the fall is at its fullest, and if you don't want to get wet on the last quarter-mile of the Mist Trail, we suggest you take along some raingear and perhaps something to keep your camera dry.

At the trailhead take the 12-foot-wide path to the left (east) of the restrooms. As you follow the trail through the open evergreen forest you'll hear the Merced River on your left.

In less than 800 feet you'll cross the cascading river on a wooden footbridge and follow the John Muir Trail to your right. The trail—mostly paved for the next mile—curves around enormous boulders, passes a tiny spring on the left and climbs steeply upstream. Oak trees grow in the cracks of the steep cliffs—the lower slopes of Grizzly Peak—on your left and the Merced roars over its rocky bed more than 100 feet below, on your right.

Less than a third of a mile from the bridge the path levels off at a stone-walled viewpoint. Here, at a cliff-edge aerie in a bend in the trail high above the Merced, you have a 200-degree view. Ahead of you, on the opposite side of the Merced, is the steep, bare slope of Panorama Cliff (Walk No. 13). To the right of the cliff is 370-foot Illilouette Fall, plunging down Illilouette Canyon. To the right of the canyon is Illilouette Ridge and 7,214-foot Glacier Point (Walk No. 8). To your right is Yosemite Valley, Upper Yosemite Fall (Walks No. 1 and 2) and, to the right of the fall, the Royal Arches. Below you are the

Bridalveil Fall *seen from the parking area for Walk No. 3.*

▶

green pools and white cascades of the turbulent Merced, twisting through the narrow, boulder-filled canyon.

You'll have more views of the Merced, as well as Panorama Cliff, Illilouette Fall and Illilouette Creek, as you continue climbing higher up the Merced canyon.

Finally, after passing over a sunny rock slide, you come to a wide wooden footbridge over the Merced. Here, .8 miles from the trailhead, you get your first look at Vernal Fall, less than half a mile upstream.

Unlike the high, thin falls in Yosemite Valley, which are fed only by creeks, Vernal is produced by the Merced River. And it shows. Instead of a dainty, diaphonous curtain, Vernal is a thick, 100-foot-wide shaft of white water. The fall drops over the edge of a nearly vertical gray granite wall that's almost twice as tall as the cataract. Left of the fall is the bare, bell-shaped 7,076-foot-high rock appropriately known as Liberty Cap. Below the fall—indeed, as far up and down the river as you can see—there is almost no part of the Merced that isn't frothy white as it dashes around gray ledges and cabin-size boulders. Downstream you can see, from left to right, Panorama Cliff, Illilouette Canyon, Illilouette Ridge, Glacier Point and, to the right of the Merced, the cliffs of Grizzly Peak.

On the other side of the bridge is an emergency telephone, a drinking fountain and a handsome fieldstone and wood building containing restrooms with flush toilets—the last such amenities on the Walk.

Now the paved trail climbs gently through the

forest, close to the south bank of the Merced, and you'll see the rushing river on your left.

In about a quarter of a mile from the bridge the trail splits: The John Muir Trail (see Walk No. 7) goes to the right; the Mist Trail continues upstream. Follow the Mist Trail for another couple of hundred feet, where a small trail on the left leads quickly to a huge, flat-topped boulder in the Merced known as Lady Franklin Rock. The rock was named for the wife of the British explorer, Sir John Franklin, after she was carried here on a litter for a view of the fall in 1859.

Here, amid panhandling squirrels and Steller's jays (which the Park Service asks you not to feed), you're only a few hundred yards from the fall and you can often feel its far-reaching spray. But the fall is only the largest cascade among thousands, large and small, that you can see crashing in a 1,000-foot stretch of the Merced that begins at the base of the fall, roars along the edge of Lady Franklin Rock and continues downstream as far as you can see. This natural water show would be remarkable anywhere else. But here it's dwarfed by the huge fall.

Ahead, on your right, on the mist-soaked bank of the river — so wet that no trees can grow on it — you can see people climbing up the stone steps toward the falls. From the rock, this .3-mile walk may look unappealing — steep, slippery and wet. Actually, it's the most exhilarating walk in the park. The carefully built stone steps provide firm footing, appropriate rain gear will keep you and your possessions as dry as you want them to be, and the feel of soft mist and the views of rainbows and falling water combine to make the walk anything but tedious. Do it! You'll love it!

From Lady Franklin Rock the trail quickly climbs out of the forest and onto a grassy slope. Ahead of you, in the center of a massive 500-foot-wide wall that bestrides the Merced like a dam, is the fall. Above you, on both sides of the river, rise the steep walls of the Merced canyon. Fifty feet below you is the foaming Merced. As you get closer to the fall, you'll feel the mist, which rises from the river like steam from a cauldron. You'll also begin to see large, wide rainbows on the misty, grassy slope.

The trail now consists of wet granite steps. Climb them slowly, both to make sure your footing is secure and to savor the views of the fall. Unlike the Walks to Yosemite and Bridalveil falls (Nos. 1-3), the Mist Trail takes you not only to the base of the fall but *beside* it — and barely a couple of hundred feet away from it. You can see how the huge, dense column of water crashes with enormous kinetic energy onto the rocks below. There's a dark green pool beneath the falls but it's hard to see it through the rainbows and the thick pile of mist rising hundreds of feet up the sides of the canyon.

Less then a third of a mile from Lady Franklin Rock, the Mist Trail reenters the woods and starts a short, steep climb to the very top of the falls. The climb is tedious and trees block the view of the

Mount Watkins, on the left, and the base of Half Dome, on the right, are delicately reflected in the glass-smooth surface of **Mirror Lake** *(Walk No. 4).* ▶

cataract, the river and the mist. The John Muir Trail (Walk No. 7), which also takes you to Nevada Fall, is an easier and more scenic way to reach the top of Vernal Fall. If you have time to take that Walk, you may want to turn around here, retrace your steps to the trailhead and enjoy the views from the opposite direction. If you *don't* plan to take Walk No. 7, now may be the time to go to the top of Vernal Fall and see the Emerald Pool and the Silver Apron, both immediately above it. See pages 62-63 for a description.

7 Nevada Fall

This moderate eight-mile round trip follows the John Muir Trail to the top of 594-foot Nevada Fall. En route you'll enjoy views of Yosemite, Illilouette and Vernal falls; the turbulent Merced River; Illilouette Ridge and Glacier Point; Half Dome and Yosemite Valley; Panorama Cliff, Grizzly Peak, Mount Broderick and Liberty Cap—all part of the rock walls of the Merced canyon—and two memorable water features: the Merced River's Silver Apron and, below it, the Emerald Pool. On your way back, you'll follow the route of Walk No. 6, which includes the exhilarating Mist Trail beside Vernal Fall.

Like the trails to Happy Isles and Vernal Fall

(Walks No. 5 and 6) this Walk begins at Shuttle Bus Stop No. 16 on the eastern end of the Yosemite Valley loop road.

Follow the route of Walk No. 6 (page 47) to the trail junction just before Lady Franklin Rock, then take the John Muir Trail to the right, away from the Merced River. You'll immediately pass to the right of a large rock overhanging the trail. Just after the rock you'll come to another junction, where a horse trail from Yosemite Valley joins the Muir Trail on the right. Stay on the Muir Trail, which starts climbing up the wall of the Merced canyon in long, gentle switchbacks.

On the very first switchback you'll begin to catch glimpses of major promontories. Directly to the south, barely 1,000 feet away, is Panorama Cliff. To the right of the cliff, on the far side of Illilouette Gorge, is Illilouette Ridge. At the end of the ridge is Glacier Point (Walk No. 8). On the opposite bank of the Merced (and on the south flank of Half Dome) is Grizzly Peak.

After the seventh switchback the view expands to include the eastern end of Yosemite Valley and Upper Yosemite Fall. Then the east, or "back," side of Half Dome comes into view. The vistas get even more expansive as you slowly climb above the Merced.

At the ninth switchback you skirt the base of Panorama Cliff.

At the 17th switchback the trail levels off. You're now several hundred feet above the Merced and you have 240-degree views. You see everything to the west that you saw on your way up plus more features

to the north and east. The white slope of Nevada Fall is below on your right. To the left of the fall, on the north side of the Merced, are three bare peaks. Closest to the fall is the 7,076-foot Liberty Cap, which is shaped exactly like its namesake. To the left of Liberty Cap, and separated from it by a deep ravine, is 6,706-foot Mount Broderick. To the left of Broderick and a mile to the north is the back side of Half Dome.

These views continue uninterrupted as you follow the nearly level cliff-top trail to the wide, sloping ledges of Clark Point. Here, almost 2.5 miles from the trailhead, you'll catch a glimpse of Emerald Pool, which is far below on your right, just above Vernal Fall.

Here, too, the trail splits again. Straight ahead is the .6-mile path to the top of Vernal Fall, which you'll take on your way back from Nevada Fall. The Muir Trail continues on the right, switching back and forth up the open ledges and offering continuous views of the landmarks of eastern Yosemite Valley and the lower Merced canyon. As you face the Merced the panorama includes, from left to right, Glacier Point, Yosemite Valley, Grizzly Peak, Half Dome, Mount Broderick, Liberty Cap and Nevada Fall.

As you get closer and closer to the fall, you'll see long swags of pure white water pouring over the

The 317-foot-high **Vernal Fall** *(Walks No. 6, 7 and 13) and walkers on the Mist Trail, at right, seen from Lady Franklin Rock.*

◀

massive gray ledge that stretches across the Merced like a dam. About halfway down the fall, the water smashes into a rock outcrop, causing it to leap horizontally into the air in what John Muir called comets or shooting stars of water. As if this weren't enough to look at, there's more: Glance to your left as you approach Nevada Fall and you'll have another view of Upper Yosemite Fall, more than four miles away.

Now the Walk becomes even more dramatic. Less than a third of a mile from the top of the fall the trail follows a shelf in the nearly vertical canyon wall that's an extension of the natural 600-foot-wide dam over which the fall drops. Here the trail is a 500-foot-long corniche, a long natural balcony from which one has continuous views of the fall and the white mist rising from below it, as well as glimpses of the canyon floor and the frothing river. On your left, at the very edge of the corniche, is a low fieldstone wall. On your right water trickles down the steep ledges, watering the wildflowers growing in the rocks. You'll actually walk *under* the ledge for about 30 feet and the water will drip on you.

Soon after the trail leaves the corniche, you'll reach the junction where the Panorama Trail (Walk No. 13) enters the Muir Trail on your right. Near the intersection is a tiny, pretty stream spilling over a ledge as it runs across the trail. An emergency telephone is here too.

Keep following the Muir Trail toward the fall. You'll have another good view of the Merced canyon, Glacier Point and Grizzly Peak on your left. About .2 miles from the trail junction, you'll reach the wide, smooth gray ledges at the top of Nevada Fall — one of the most exciting rock-and-water compositions in the park.

On your right, above the fall, the Merced cascades noisily around a low island and flows into a large, ledge-bottomed, blue-green pool. Then the river becomes a churning, foaming mass as it surges through a 20-foot-wide chute in the ledge and plunges over the edge of the rock dam. So turbulent is the river here that it creates mist even before it falls. Cross the sturdy wood and steel bridge over the river and get a close, bird's-eye view of one of the wildest bits of river in Yosemite.

On the north side of the bridge, stroll along the ledges beside the pools upstream. For a close view of the fall, walk along the ledge on the north side of the cataract until you come to the metal pipe railing and stone steps leading down to a viewpoint at the very top of the fall. Here you can see huge, white billows — part air, part water — surging down the ledge chute with such force that they don't fall as much as leap off the ledge. Below the fall, in the bottom of the canyon, the river is so white it looks like milk and mist rises like white smoke. Downstream, between the walls of the narrow, steep-sided canyon, you can glimpse the Emerald Pool, just above Vernal Fall. Above the pool, to the left, are the slopes of Panorama Cliff. To the right of the cliff, rising into the notch of the canyon, is Glacier Point. To the right of the point, sticking straight up above the shoulder of Half Dome, is Grizzly Peak. Directly to your right and rising 1,000 feet above you is the bare rock of Liberty Cap. To the left of Liberty Cap is Mount

Broderick.

The ledges above Nevada Fall are the halfway point of the Walk and a perfect spot for a rest, a snack or a picnic.

When you're ready to continue, retrace your steps to Clark Point and take a right onto the .6-mile path that descends to Vernal Falls. The trail switches back and forth, first over open ledges, then through oaks and evergreens, as it drops deeper and deeper into the gorge.

About halfway down the trail, you suddenly find yourself at one of the best-situated vantage points in the park. You are now both in front of and *above* Vernal Fall and the scene before you is from a 19th-century American landscape painting. Below you, above the fall, the Merced runs past low, rocky islands, slides transparently over wide, smooth ledges, then turns white as it falls in gossamer swags across the huge rock outcrop that spans the canyon like a dam. The water smashes on rocks and into a dark, emerald-green pool below, and mist shoots out in all directions, soaking the lush green grass along the south slope of the canyon and wetting the evergreens on the north slope. The wet, treeless terrain looks more like Ireland than the Sierra Nevada. The fall makes so much mist that it sometimes rises as high as the overlook you're standing on. Above the fall you can see the Emerald Pool. Further upstream you can even see Nevada Fall. Tiny-looking people

One of many rainbows below the Mist Trail to **Vernal Fall**
(Walks No. 6, 7 and 13). ▶

stand on the dry part of the ledge at the top of Vernal Fall, dwarfed by the cataract and everything around them. To help them make nature appear vast and powerful, 19th-century American landscape painters drew very small people in very big landscapes on enormous canvases. They would have loved the scene below.

As you keep following the trail down to the fall you'll catch glimpses of the Silver Apron, above Emerald Pool.

The trail ends at the Mist Trail on a ledgy area near the Merced. Take a right at the junction and follow the Mist Trail upstream. In about .1 miles you'll reach a steel bridge over the river. From there you can see the Merced flowing frothy white through a narrow flume in the ledge. Downstream is the Silver Apron, a 60-foot-wide, 200-foot-long ledge over which the Merced flows in countless tiny cascades. You may also see people on the flat ledge "beach" beside the cascades. Upstream, through the steep gorge, you can see Mount Broderick, Liberty Cap and the top of Nevada Fall.

Go back to the trail junction and keep following the Mist Trail down stone steps. Very soon you'll see the Silver Apron through the evergreens. Leave the trail, walk about 50 feet to the river and you'll be beside one of the most unusual rock-and-water formations in the world. Here the Merced flows shallowly over ledge like the end of a wave lapping on a stony beach. Thousands of tiny jets of water erupt all over the ledge in a strange, mesmerizing display.

Upstream, as foam flies into the air, the Merced pours out of the gorge underneath the steel bridge, then cascades over ledges on both banks of the river just above the Silver Apron. You can often see rainbows at the bottom of the ledges.

Below the Silver Apron the river slides over ledge and crashes into the Emerald Pool, making white waves in the green water. The 100-foot-wide, 200-foot-long pool is one of the largest sheets of smooth water on any stream in the park. On the opposite bank of the pool, smooth, flat ledges slope into the water like beaches made of rock instead of sand.

The Merced flows turbulently over rocks for another 100 feet or so before it glides transparently over more smooth ledge at the top of the fall and then roars over the edge in a wide, thick, pure white column of water. Downstream the churning river is milky white. Panorama Cliff rises on the left, Grizzly Peak on the right. Mount Broderick and Liberty Cap are behind you.

You watch this watery vista from behind a pipe fence that runs along the edge of a wide, flat triangle of ledge at the very top of the fall. When you're ready to continue, follow the metal fence away from the river, up the sloping ledge. The fence will lead you immediately to a metal gate at the top of the ledge. Go through the gate and follow the stone steps down the sheer cliff, which is part of the natural "dam" creating Vernal Fall. The steps will quickly take you down through the trees to where the Mist Trail is soaked by spray from the fall. This point is the climax of the Walk to Vernal Fall (Walk No. 6). From here you follow the return route of Walk No. 6, which takes you back to the trailhead near Happy Isles. See pages 47-52 for directions and

a description of what you'll see on the way.

8 Glacier Point

This easy half-mile round trip takes you along the rim of an overlook 3,000 feet above Yosemite Valley. No place in the park offers a better bird's-eye view of the valley. In fact, few other places in the world offer such awesome vistas for so little effort.

Glacier Point is on top of the south wall of Yosemite Valley and at the end of the Glacier Point Road, 26 miles from the intersection of the valley loop road and the Wawona Road in the western end of the valley. (See pages 20-21 for a description of the sights along the Glacier Point Road.)

The road ends in a large paved parking area about .2 miles from Glacier Point. Follow the wide, nearly level asphalt path toward the point. You'll quickly pass the restrooms (which have running water and flush toilets), on the right. Immediately after the restrooms the trail forks. Go right.

As you walk past the gift shop and snack bar on your left, a stunning panorama opens on your right. In the distance, on the far right, are the peaks of the Clark Range, snow covered even in late summer.

The 594-foot-high **Nevada Fall** *seen from the John Muir Trail (Walks No. 7 and 13).*
◄

Left of the Clark Range and rising almost a mile above Illilouette Gorge is 9,092-foot Mount Starr King. Left of Starr King is Panorama Cliff (see Walk No. 13), which drops steeply down to the narrow, deep canyon of the Merced River. At the bottom of the canyon is the long, thin milk-white ribbon of the cascading river and two falls: Vernal (Walk No. 6) and, above it, Nevada (Walk No. 7). Although the falling water is more than two miles away you can hear it clearly in the spring and early summer, when it is flowing fullest. Left of the falls is the bare rock sugarloaf called Liberty Cap. Left of Liberty Cap is Mount Broderick. Rising to the left of the Merced canyon is the tallest thing you can see on the edge of Yosemite Valley: the massive smooth gray rock hulk of Half Dome. Left of Half Dome is Tenaya Canyon and Mirror Lake (Walk No. 4). On the north wall of Tenaya Canyon are, from right to left: 8,500-foot Mount Watkins, 7,612-foot Basket Dome and 7,542-foot North Dome.

Barely 500 feet from the parking area, you'll come to the very rim of the valley and to a small, handsome fieldstone structure known as the "geology exhibit." Inside this open, gazebolike building are plaques explaining how the valley was created by glaciers. From here you can also see the concentric Royal Arches on the valley's north wall and, left of the arches, Yosemite Falls (Walks No. 1 and 2).

Nevada Fall *seen from the John Muir Trail (Walks No. 7 and 13). Liberty Cap is to the left.* ▶

Follow the path around the geology exhibit and out to Glacier Point. Here you'll find a stone-walled viewpoint from which you can see everything from Yosemite Falls on your left to Half Dome on your right, to Mount Hoffmann and peaks of the Cathedral Range in the distance north of the valley, to the flat forested valley floor almost directly below you.

At this 7,214-foot lookout your sense of Yosemite Valley is vastly different from what it was more than 3,000 feet below. From the valley floor, Yosemite seems to be composed of streams, meadows and towering trees. Up here the trees look no taller than an unmowed lawn and Yosemite seems to be made of nothing but towering, massive gray granite. *So* much rock. From this perspective the meadows and forests are just a green carpet at the bottom of the rock walls; the low green flatness emphasizes, in contrast, the soaring gray near-verticality of the rock. At twilight the valley's nearly level green floor sometimes looks like the sea, with Half Dome a massive stone island rising out of it. So many and so massive are the domes and stone promontories seen from Glacier Point that Yosemite appears to be not so much a valley as a giant natural sculpture garden.

The view from Glacier Point is so extraordinary and so accessible that it's worth returning to again and again. Whenever you're on the Glacier Point Road—on your way, perhaps, from Sentinel Dome or Taft Point or the Four-Mile Trail (Walks No. 9-11)—consider having a picnic supper and watching the light of the setting sun bathe Half Dome in a golden glow.

When you're ready to return to your car, follow the trail back to the parking lot and enjoy the panorama all over again. (Don't take the path that splits off the trail on the right, a few yards from Glacier Point, and rejoins the trail just before the restrooms. That route, which provides handicapped access to the point, has no views.)

9 Sentinel Dome

This moderate 2.2-mile round trip takes you higher above Yosemite Valley than any other Great Walk. From the top of 8,122-foot Sentinel Dome you have unobstructed views in all directions. The vistas include a 180-degree panorama of major landmarks that rivals the view from Glacier Point; it sweeps all the way from El Capitan and Cathedral Rocks in the west to the snow-capped Clark Range in the southeast.

Both the Walk to Sentinel Dome and the Walk to Taft Point (No. 10) begin at a parking area on the west side of the Glacier Point Road, about 23 miles from the intersection of the Yosemite Valley loop road and the Wawona Road in the western end of the valley. The parking area is also about three miles from Glacier Point and just a few hundred feet after you see Sentinel Dome from your car, on the left. (See pages 20-21 for a description of other sights

along the Glacier Point Road.)

The trail descends from the parking lot and splits in about 60 feet. The left fork goes to Taft Point. The right fork goes through open, mainly evergreen woods to Sentinel Dome.

Take the trail to the right and you'll almost immediately cross a wooden footbridge over a gently cascading tributary of Sentinel Creek. The creek is the source of Sentinel Falls, which flow 2,000 feet down the wall of Yosemite Valley in a crease by Sentinel Rock.

The trail then traverses a manzanita-covered slope. Ahead are nearly constant views of Sentinel Dome and the evergreen-dotted upper north wall of Yosemite Valley.

The trail climbs slightly as it approaches the smooth, nearly bare dome. The front of the dome is so flat that it looks as if it has just been sliced away. From here you can see the top of 7,569-foot El Capitan on the north wall of the valley.

The trail next crosses ledge and is marked with cairns (small piles of stones) and steel signs as it comes to within a few hundred feet of the dome. From here the dome looks a bit like a side view of a whale, head on the right and tail on the left. The rock is about 250 feet high and about 1,000 feet wide

---

Vernal Fall *seen from the overlook on the path linking the Mist Trail and Clark Point, on the John Muir Trail (Walk No. 7). From this unique vantage point, which is both above and in front of the cataract, you can see walkers to the right of the top of the fall.*

◄

at its base. If you can see miniature people on the top, you'll get a vivid sense of its size.

The trail now enters cool evergreen woods and passes through a parklike setting of large, handsome chinquapin bushes (whose leaves have yellow undersides) as it curves around the east side of the dome. Through the trees on your right you can see the snow-covered summits of the Clark Range; there's a comfortable 1 1/2-foot-thick log on which you can sit and enjoy the view.

The trail now follows the remains of a paved road on which tourists once drove to the base of the dome. As you climb gently toward the north side of the dome Half Dome and the top of Nevada Fall (Walk No. 7) will be visible on your right.

When the trail reaches the north side of the dome it doesn't head left and up the dome, as you might expect. Instead it makes a hairpin turn to the right and keeps curving to the right until it makes a small loop. To get to the top of the dome, you have to leave the trail and pick your own route up the north side of the rock — which, happily, has the most gentle grades on the dome. The nearly bare slope may look daunting but it's less than .1 miles to the top and you can tailor your route and your pace to suit your needs. An indirect, zigzagging approach is much easier than a direct one so go slowly and don't go straight up. Traverse the slope diagonally and make switchbacks. Above all, stop often, not only to rest but to look back and enjoy the ever-changing view, which expands with literally every step you take.

As you start your climb, turn around and you'll already see Upper Yosemite Fall (Walks No. 1 and

2) and North and Basket domes on top of Yosemite's north wall. On your left you'll see the long, flat slope of Mount Starr King and the Clark Range to its right. Then El Capitan and Cathedral Rocks, both to the left of Yosemite Fall, come into view. Next you see the bare, 8,842-foot rock massif of Half Dome and, to its left, the almost surrealistically wide, flat, smooth slope of Clouds Rest, whose sharp, long, ridgelike summit is 9,926 feet high. Soon you'll see the Middle Cascades of Yosemite Falls and the lower fall as well. You're now so high above the falls that you can see down into the crooked crags of the Middle Cascades — it's the best view of these usually hidden water features on any Great Walk. From this height you also appreciate the radical contrast between Yosemite Falls and Yosemite's walls. From here the gossamer-thin white water of the upper fall, which breaks apart and melts into air as it drifts down, could not appear softer, more fragile or more ephemeral. In contrast, the vast, gray rock behind it could not appear harder, more solid or more permanent.

More sights await you when you reach the flat top of the dome. A round plaque atop a rock illustrates the landmarks you see all around you. From right to left, beginning in the southeast, are Merced Peak, Red Peak, Gray Peak and Mount Clark, all more than 11,000 feet high, in the Clark Range, more than ten miles away; 9,092-foot Mount Starr King, four miles away and in front of Mount Clark; Nevada Fall, Little Yosemite Valley behind it and Liberty Cap to the left; 12,561-foot Mount Florence; 12,960-foot Mount Maclure, the third highest peak in the park; and 13,114-foot Mount Lyell, the park's highest peak, all on the Sierra Crest at the park's southeastern boundary, some 16 miles away. Then come Half Dome; Clouds Rest; Tenaya Peak and the Echo Peaks in the Cathedral Range, 16 miles to the northeast; Mount Watkins, its right side so flat it looks as if it had been sliced off; 12,590-foot Mount Conness, on the Sierra Crest at the northeast boundary of the park, 22 miles away; Basket Dome and North Dome; 10,850-foot Mount Hoffmann, ten miles away in the geographical center of the park; Yosemite Point; Yosemite Falls; El Capitan and Cathedral Rocks. On a clear day, you can see even more snow-topped peaks of the Sierra Crest on the edge of the park to the east and northeast.

Walk around the perimeter of the flat top of the dome and create your own panoramic views. A bit south of the plaque is the dome's legendary Jeffrey pine. Though killed in the drought of 1975-77 its gnarled and twisted trunk still stands, mute evidence of the strong wind that sometimes whips across this exposed summit.

When you're ready to return to your car, simply retrace your steps to the parking lot.

Vernal Fall (Walks No. 6, 7 and 13), left, and Nevada Fall (Walks No. 7 and 13), seen from **Glacier Point** *(Walks No. 8 and 11-13). Liberty Cap is to the left of Nevada Fall, Little Yosemite Valley is behind Liberty Cap and the snowy Sierra Crest is on the horizon.* ▶

10 Taft Point

This undemanding 2.2-mile round trip takes you through open, sunny woods to the rim of Yosemite Valley, where you have views of Cathedral Rocks, Cathedral Spires, El Capitan, the Three Brothers, Yosemite Falls and Profile Cliff. You'll also see the deep but narrow chasms in Taft Point known as the "fissures."

Like the trip to Sentinel Dome (Walk No. 9), this Walk begins at a parking area on the west side of the Glacier Point Road, about 23 miles from the intersection of the Wawona Road and the Yosemite Valley loop road.

The trail goes down from the parking lot for about 60 feet and then forks. The right path goes to Sentinel Dome, the left to Taft Point. The wide, smooth trail descends gently through a field where wildflowers bloom.

Very soon you'll come to an unusual outcrop of white quartz, on your right. Then the trail crosses gently flowing Sentinel Creek on large rocks. (The creek enters Yosemite Valley less than a mile to the north as 2,000-foot-high Sentinel Falls.) Now the path runs through an open, sunny forest of fir, pine, chinquapin and manzanita.

About .5 miles from the parking area, near a large Jeffrey pine (Jeffrey pines have a jigsaw-puzzlelike bark that smells like vanilla), the trail forks again. Go left. You'll immediately cross a tiny creek on stones and follow it briefly downstream. Drifts of wildflowers grow along the stream. The trail then moves away from the creek and gradually descends to Taft Point.

As you reach the point, you'll see the north wall of Yosemite Valley ahead and you'll pass to the left of the half-dozen fissures on the east rim of Taft Point. Some of the cracks are 40 feet long and 20 feet wide at the top and 100 feet deep at the edge of the point. Here the wall of Yosemite Valley is not merely steep or sheer but actually *overhangs* the steep, narrow ravine below it. In fact, if you crawl—carefully—to the edge of the point here and look over the rim, you'll see the bottom of the ravine and your head will be over the *opposite* (east) side of the creek running below you (the one you crossed less than half a mile back) and over the steep, evergreen-festooned slope on the *far side* of the creek. You'll also see, above the slope, the sheer walls of Profile Cliff. There are no railings along the fissures, so be careful when you're near them and keep an eye on children.

The path climbs gently, past chinquapin and pine and over ledges, to the northern edge of Taft Point. Here an iron pipe fence marks the front and sides of a tiny six-foot-wide, three-foot-deep overlook on the rim of Yosemite Valley. Swallows streak by like tiny jets at amazing speeds. A US Geological Survey marker states that you are now 7,503 feet above sea level. More than 3,500 feet below are light green meadows, dark green forests and the meandering Merced River on the long, narrow valley floor. On the opposite wall of the valley and to your left is the

smooth, buttresslike cliff of 7,569-foot El Capitan. Note how a dark patch of diorite on its face is shaped like a map of North America. With help from binoculars you may also be able to see climbers maneuvering upward. To the right of El Capitan and almost directly across the valley are the promontories known as the Three Brothers: from left to right, the Lower Brother, the slightly higher Middle Brother and 7,779-foot Eagle Peak, the highest brother of all. To the right of the Brothers are the long white ribbons of Yosemite Falls (Walks No. 1 and 2). To the right of the falls and ten miles away, in the geographical center of the park, is 10,850-foot Mount Hoffmann. To the right of Hoffmann and almost 24 miles away, on the Sierra Crest, is 12,590-foot Mount Conness, snowcapped even in late summer.

From this snug perch, follow a sandy path past large balanced rocks out to the western edge of the point, where your view widens dramatically. Now you can see down the western end of the valley. Cathedral Rocks and the Cathedral Spires rise above the south wall of the valley, their prickly-pointed tops echoing the pointed evergreens below them. To your left Taft Point drops into a deep ravine. To your far right you can see Sentinel Rock to the north (left) of Profile Cliff. Be careful here because there's no barrier on the edge of the point.

When you're ready to return to your car, retrace

A host of shooting stars in bloom in Summit Meadow, on the road to **Glacier Point** *(Walks No. 8 and 11-13).*
◄

your route to the parking area.

11 Four-Mile Trail (I)

This undemanding mile-long round trip along the rim of Yosemite Valley offers clear views of many natural landmarks, including Little Yosemite Valley, Vernal Fall, the Emerald Pool, the Silver Apron, Half Dome, Clouds Rest, Tenaya Canyon, Mirror Meadow, Mount Watkins, Basket Dome, North Dome, the Washington Column, the Royal Arches, Yosemite Falls, El Capitan, Cathedral Rocks, Sentinel Rock and almost all of the Yosemite Valley floor.

The Walk begins in the Glacier Point parking area at the end of the Glacier Point Road. Follow the paved trail leading to the point and turn to page 65 (Walk No. 8) for a description of the panoramic view.

Immediately after passing the restrooms the trail forks. Go left. About 100 feet after the fork, the trail splits again. Go left again and follow the now un-paved trail between three- to six-foot-thick ever-greens.

The wide, smooth path makes a quick, steep descent to a tiny stream flowing down the middle of a long, narrow meadow. The green meadow is a linear focal point on the brown forest floor. You cross the stream on stones and the trail, now nearly level, starts to traverse the valley wall.

Soon views open up through the trees on the right of the path. You'll see the Royal Arches on the north wall of the valley and, above them, 7,542-foot North Dome and, to the right of North Dome, 7,612-foot Basket Dome.

Gradually the trail moves closer to the valley rim and the trees thin out. Ledges rise steeply on the left side of the trail. On the right the rock slope plunges even more precipitously and long, steep rock spurs alternate with long, deep, narrow ravines. Soon you can see landmarks at the eastern end of the valley. Tenaya Canyon comes into view at your right rear. On the north side of the canyon is Mount Watkins. On the south side is Half Dome and Clouds Rest.

Next you'll glimpse the valley floor, then snow-capped High Sierra peaks in the distance and, to your rear, the rocks of Glacier Point thrusting out over Yosemite Valley. With binoculars you can pick out people on the point.

As the trail goes farther and farther to the north you can see past Glacier Point and up the Merced canyon to Vernal Fall, the Emerald Pool and the Silver Apron (Walks No. 6-7). Use your binoculars again to spot people on top of the fall. Upstream, you'll also see the flat, bare rock walls of Little Yosemite Valley.

Next you'll see Mirror Meadow (Walk No. 4) in Tenaya Canyon. Then you'll have one of the best views anywhere of Yosemite Falls (Walks No. 1-2), which is across the valley, less than two miles away. You're close enough to hear the falls and high enough to have a rare view of the long ribbon of white water winding through the crags of the Middle Cascades.

About a quarter-mile from the trailhead the path becomes a wide shelf carved into the steep valley wall and supported on the right by stone walls. You now have a continuous view of the Yosemite Valley floor and its north wall all the way from Yosemite Falls in the west to Tenaya Canyon and Clouds Rest in the east. Go slowly here and savor the rare uninterrupted panorama on your right.

About .5 miles from the trailhead the trail curves to the left around the steep valley wall and then switches back sharply to the right. Here you suddenly come upon one of the best vistas of the west valley. Below you the Merced gleams in the sun as it meanders westward through the El Capitan Meadow and the forests beyond. To the right of the river, the smooth monolith of 7,569-foot El Capitan rises almost straight up from the north side of the valley. Left of the river, and just half a mile away, are the nearly vertical cliffs of 7,038-foot Sentinel Rock and, on top of the rock, a ridge prickly with sharp, jagged rocks and pointed evergreen trees. Together, El Capitan and Sentinel Rock, the highest points in front of you, make a near-vertical frame for the picture of the valley between them. To the right of Sentinel Rock and more than three miles down the valley, Cathedral Rocks rise steeply a half-mile

The setting sun at **Glacier Point** *(Walks No. 8 and 11) makes Half Dome glow. Clouds Rest is to the left.* ►

above the trees on the valley floor. These high, hard, wonderfully rugged vertical rocks contrast dramatically with the soft, low, delicate-looking green meadows and forests on the valley floor.

This viewpoint is perhaps the best one on the trail. It's a fit place for a rest, a snack or even a picnic before you turn around and return to Glacier Point.

12 Four-Mile Trail (II)

This moderate one-way Walk, actually 4.8 miles long, begins by following the route of Walk No. 11 and takes you all the way down the Four-Mile Trail, from the top of Yosemite Valley to the bottom. Along the way you'll have views of Little Yosemite Valley, Vernal Falls, the Emerald Pool, the Silver Apron, Half Dome, Clouds Rest, Tenaya Canyon, Mirror Meadow, Mount Watkins, Basket Dome, North Dome, the Washington Column, the Royal Arches, El Capitan, Cathedral Rocks, the Cathedral Spires, Sentinel Rock and almost all of Yosemite Valley (and the Merced River) plus frequent vistas of Yosemite Falls from several angles and many altitudes.

The Walk is one way because you ride the tour bus from Yosemite Lodge to Glacier Point. (See page 22 for more information on the bus service.)

After you get off the bus at the Glacier Point

parking area follow the description of Walk No. 11, which begins on page 80. But instead of turning around at the half-mile point of Walk No. 11, keep following the trail as it switches sharply back to the right and keeps switching back and forth down the valley. As you pass through manzanita, chinquapin and evergreen trees you'll have frequent, often continuous views of North Dome, Yosemite Falls, Sentinel Rock, Cathedral Rocks, the Cathedral Spires, El Capitan and the Merced River meandering through the flat, green floor of western Yosemite Valley.

About halfway down the trail, as you head east on a relatively long, nearly level switchback across a manzanita- and chinquapin-covered flat, look for a (usually) unmarked trail on your left. The three-foot-wide path leads you, in about 50 feet, to a clearing and, in a few more feet, to a tiny overlook between two rocks that's framed by a six-foot-long iron pipe fence. This is Union Point. And the view from this little-visited overlook is as good as any on the Four-Mile Trail. Before you, from left to right, are Yosemite Falls—here less than a mile and a half away—the Royal Arches, the Washington Column, North Dome, Mount Watkins, Tenaya Canyon, Clouds Rest and Half Dome. In the bottom of the valley is Leidig Meadow; Yosemite Lodge is on the right.

Retrace your steps to the Four-Mile Trail and follow it down through a steep ravine. You'll see North Dome, Mount Watkins and Clouds Rest again. As the trail climbs out of the ravine and heads west, you'll have an excellent view of Half Dome and another view of Sentinel Rock and Cathedral Rocks.

Then the trail switches back and forth below Union Point, providing still more views of Yosemite Falls, Sentinel and Cathedral rocks, North Dome, Clouds Rest and Half Dome.

Now the trail becomes more level as it heads west, below Sentinel Rock. Manzanita and chinquapin are gradually replaced by oaks, which obscure the views, and you have only glimpses of Sentinel Rock, Yosemite Falls, Leidig Meadow and the sandbars in the Merced.

About three miles from the trailhead the trail crosses a small stream flowing over large rocks in a ravine. Sentinel Rock now looms high on your left and Cathedral Rock is ahead.

After passing through oaks and big-leaf maples the trail switches sharply back to the right and runs through an evergreen forest as it approaches the valley loop road.

If you took the bus to Glacier Point and want to go back to Yosemite Lodge to pick up your car, take a right on the path that runs parallel to the loop road. You'll soon see a parking area and an evergreen-shaded picnic area on the other side of the road. Carefully cross the road and walk through the picnic area. You'll quickly come to a paved bicycle path

---

Sentinel Dome (*Walk No. 9*) *provides the highest view of Yosemite Falls on any Great Walk. From this 8,122-foot summit you can see not only the upper and lower falls but also the Middle Cascades.* ▶

that crosses the Merced on a wooden bridge. Cross the river — notice its unusually smooth gravel bed — and follow the paved path back to Yosemite Lodge, about .5 miles away.

13 Panorama Trail

Like the Four-Mile Trail, this moderate 8.5-mile one-way Walk takes you from the top of Yosemite Valley to the bottom. It starts at Glacier Point, winds down Illilouette Ridge, crosses Illilouette Gorge, climbs along the top of Panorama Cliff, descends to the top of Nevada Fall and then follows the route of Walk No. 6 or 7 (your choice) down to Happy Isles. Along the way you'll have many views of nearly two dozen natural features, including the Royal Arches, North Dome, Basket Dome, Mount Watkins, Tenaya Canyon, Mirror Lake, Half Dome, Grizzly Peak, the Merced River, Mount Broderick, Liberty Cap, Yosemite, Vernal, Nevada and Illilouette falls, Illilouette Creek, Panorama Cliff, Mount Starr King, the Clark Range and Glacier Point.

Like Walk No. 12, this Walk is one way because you ride the tour bus to Glacier Point from Yosemite Lodge and, on your return trip, take the Shuttle Bus from Happy Isles back to the lodge. (See pages 18 and 22 for more information on both bus services.) It's a moderate Walk because it goes steadily downhill with only about a mile of climbing. However, some of the climbing is done on sunny slopes and, if the weather's hot, the Walk can be tedious and sweaty; so try to go on a cool day or start early in the morning, when the temperature is lower.

After you get off the bus at the Glacier Point parking area follow the wide asphalt path leading to the point and turn to page 65 (Walk No. 8) for a description of the panoramic view.

Between the restrooms and the gift shop, an unpaved, stone-bordered trail branches off to the right. Follow this wide path up the bare slope. In a couple of hundred feet the trail forks. Go left and follow the smooth, sandy trail down the wooded east slope of Illilouette Ridge. First the trail switches gently back and forth; then it traverses the wooded east slope of the ridge as it gradually descends into Illilouette Gorge.

A forest fire swept through here in 1986, so the woods are open. Through the fire-blackened trees on your left you'll have 90-degree views. Mount Watkins and Mirror Meadow in Tenaya Canyon (Walk No. 4) and Half Dome are to the northeast. The gray-brown cone of Mount Starr King and the snowy summits of the Clark Range and the Sierra Crest are in the southeast. In the middle of the vista is the milky-white Merced River, tumbling down its narrow canyon. Vernal and Nevada falls pour over gray cliffs that span the river like natural dams. Framing the river are smooth, nearly vertical evergreen-dotted natural rock sculptures: Grizzly Peak,

Mount Broderick and Liberty Cap, on the left of the falls, and Panorama Cliff, on the right.

As you traverse the slope of Illilouette Ridge the panoramas widen. You'll see North Dome above the north wall of Yosemite Valley and you'll catch a glimpse of Illilouette Fall and Illilouette Creek in the gorge less than half a mile to your left. Farther on you'll start hearing the fall.

About a mile from the trailhead the trail splits again. Go left. The roar of Illilouette Fall will get louder and louder as the trail switches back and forth down the gorge.

The switchbacks stop at an overlook above Illilouette Creek, two miles from Glacier Point. The scene is a dramatic study in verticality. In front of you is deep, rocky Illilouette Gorge. Across the gorge is 370-foot Illilouette Fall, which flows through a tiny notch on the rim and almost immediately spreads out like a horse's tail. Then the fall drops in long, pointed swags of white water before running in long, elegant streaks down the wall of the steep gorge and splashing on the rocks below, creating mist and rainbows at the bottom of the gorge. Behind the fall you can see Half Dome and Panorama Cliff. The total vertical distance from the top of Half Dome to the bottom of the gorge—the highest and lowest points in the vista—is almost 3,500 feet.

Half Dome and, behind it, Clouds Rest, seen from **Sentinel Dome** *(Walk No. 9). The red wildflowers are mountain pride penstemon.*
◀

As the trail keeps descending to Illilouette Creek, it crosses a refreshing water feature: a tiny creek trickling prettily down a long mossy ledge on the right of the trail, with western azaleas growing nearby.

By now, signs of the forest fire have disappeared. The trail runs through lush, shady evergreens as it passes several campsites on the banks of Illilouette Creek.

Then the path crosses the creek on an 80-foot-long steel bridge. From the bridge you can see the wide stream cascading over broad, smooth, sun-bleached ledges into a blue-green pool.

From the other side of the creek you have good views, to your left, of the smooth, steep, gray walls of Illilouette Ridge and the observation platform on top of the cliff where you were a few minutes ago. (Binoculars will make these views even better.)

As you start climbing up Panorama Cliff, you'll see more of the foaming Illilouette Creek and the top of Illilouette Fall, as well as North Dome, Basket Dome and the Royal Arches on the north wall of Yosemite Valley.

The views disappear briefly as the trail switches back and forth through manzanita, then under shady evergreens as it slowly ascends Panorama Cliff.

Soon, however, the trail roughly parallels the edge of the cliff as it keeps climbing through open, sunny woods of evergreen trees and manzanita. Through the trees you'll still catch views of Half Dome, the Royal Arches and North and Basket domes. You'll also get ever-widening views of Yosemite Valley.

Upper Yosemite Fall, then the lower fall, then the steep slope of Glacier Point will all come into view.

The trail swings briefly away from the cliff top, into the woods and away from views. Then it returns to the edge of the cliff, levels off and offers vistas of the back sides of Half Dome and Clouds Rest, as well as Mount Broderick, Liberty Cap and, briefly, Nevada Fall.

About four miles from the trailhead the trail splits again — go left. Then it starts switching back and forth down to the top of Nevada Fall. Now you'll see, from right to left, the ledges and the smooth, dark water above the fall, the narrow sluiceway of white water on top of the cataract, and the huge white fall pouring over the cliff.

You'll walk over bits of asphalt — the vestige of old paving — as the trail crosses tiny streams trickling over large sunny ledges and mossy rocks. Note the rock walls built to keep water off the trail.

About 1,000 feet from the fall the trail joins the John Muir Trail. From this junction follow the description of Walk No. 7 (Nevada Fall) on pages 58-65 as you walk toward the fall and then four miles back to Shuttle Bus Stop No. 16 near Happy Isles. On your way back to Happy Isles you have a choice: At Clark Point you can continue following the route of Walk No. 7 (by walking down to Vernal Fall and taking the Mist Trail back to the John Muir Trail) or you can take the route of Walk No. 7 in reverse by staying on the Muir Trail all the way back to Happy Isles. Both routes are downhill and both are filled with spectacular views. Check the description of Walk No. 7 to see which scenery you'd most like to

see. If you've taken or plan to take Walk No. 6 but not Walk No. 7 we suggest you stay on the Muir Trail, as this will be your only chance to see the panoramic views on that route.

14 Mariposa Grove

This undemanding excursion takes you on foot through the densest concentrations of mature giant sequoias in the largest giant sequoia grove in the park. You'll see the biggest trees in the grove as well as dozens of other sequoias that are as wide as rooms. The outing includes an easy .8-mile walk, a moderate three-mile walk that offers a panoramic view of Wawona, and two 2.5-mile open-air tram rides through the grove, on which the drivers explain how the sequoias live long enough to become the world's largest living organisms. If you're short of time, you can walk just a little or even not at all and still see a large number of sequoias from the tram.

The Mariposa Grove is two miles from the park's

The Merced River and Yosemite Valley seen from the **Four-Mile Trail** *(Walks No. 11 and 12). The jagged peaks of Sentinel Rock are on the left, El Capitan is on the right and Cathedral Rocks are beyond Sentinel Rock.*
◀

south entrance station and seven miles from Wawona. As you drive into the grove you'll pass through a group of five giant sequoias known as the Sentinels. Then you'll immediately come to a parking loop that runs around two more giant sequoias. (One tree has been burned out so badly that what's left of its base looks like flying buttresses on a Gothic cathedral.) Near the entrance to the parking lot are restrooms with chemical toilets, a gift shop that also sells ice cream and drinks, and a kiosk where you buy tickets for the tram tour. The gift shop also sells the *Mariposa Grove of Giant Sequoias Guide and Map,* published by the Yosemite Association, and the colorful *Map & Guide to Wawona & the Mariposa Grove of Big Trees,* published by Rufus Graphics. Both pamphlets are modestly priced and they describe, among other things, the named trees in the grove and they show you where these trees are. The second publication has an especially good map of the grove.

Start your trip by boarding an open-air tram. (They run from about late April to mid-October, depending on snow conditions; in the summer they run all day and leave every 20 minutes.) As the tram takes you from the Lower Grove to the Upper Grove, which has the densest concentration of giant sequoias in the park, you'll pass almost a dozen

Clockwise from lower right: 370-foot Illilouette Fall, Illilouette Creek, Half Dome, the canyon of the Merced River and Panorama Cliff seen from the **Panorama Trail** *(Walk No. 13).* ▶

named trees that your driver will describe, including such curiosities as the Clothespin Tree and the Faithful Couple.

The tram stops at the Mariposa Grove Museum (a drinking fountain and flush toilets are nearby). Get off here, check out the exhibits in the rustic, one-story log-cabin museum and begin a three-mile walking tour of the Upper Grove, where you can see giant sequoias in almost every direction. (You'll return to the museum later to ride the tram back to the parking area.)

Follow the loop road east from the museum (in the opposite direction from which the tram was traveling). In about 100 feet you'll see a trail on the left and a sign saying that the Telescope Tree is .3 miles away. The trail will take you quickly uphill, through drifts of ceanothus bushes, to the Stable Tree, on the right of the path. A sign beside the tree, which fell in 1934, explains that "during the days of stagecoach travel, mangers were built in the semicircular fire scar of this tree."

The trail keeps ascending gently, past other giant sequoias, until it climbs up onto the loop road on wooden steps. The Telescope Tree is on the other side of the road. Fire has hollowed out so much of this giant that you can walk inside, look up and see the sky through its crown. Amazingly, despite all it's been through, this tree is still alive.

Find the trail behind the Telescope Tree and follow it up the slope, away from the road. In about 100 feet you'll come to the trail that runs parallel to the road. Go left at the intersection and, as you follow the smooth, almost level path, enjoy the sequoias on both sides of the trail.

Less than .5 miles from the Telescope Tree the trail switches back to the left and rejoins the road. On your right you'll see the Galen Clark Tree, named after Yosemite's first "guardian" or superintendent. This tree is supposed to be the first sequoia Clark saw when he discovered the grove in 1857. At this point the tram road curves to the left and the .5-mile road to Wawona Point goes straight ahead.

Cars used to be allowed on the paved roads in the grove but the Park Service decided that the sequoias would be better off without them and in 1969 it barred them from the grove. Now walkers share the main roads only with the trams and the road to Wawona Point only with each other. Follow the latter as it climbs steeply, switches back to the right, then back to the left and emerges at a former parking area. From here stone steps lead down to a paved, gently curving, 100-foot-long overlook.

Stroll along this 6,810-foot-high viewpoint and enjoy the 180-degree view. Almost 2,800 feet below is the mile-long Wawona Meadow and Golf Course, which from here seems to be shaped like a seahorse. On your right are the bare cliffs of 6,899-foot Wawona Dome. In a ravine left of the dome is the long, barely perceptible ribbon of Chilnualna Creek. On your left is the valley of the South Fork of the Merced River, which flows away from you, to the north. Rising to the right of the valley and running parallel to the overlook is Turner Ridge. Rising to the left of, and parallel to, the valley are the Chowchilla Mountains. On your far left is 5,762-foot Mount Savage and, southwest of Savage, the bare rock slopes of Hogan Mountain and Bald Rock. Wawona Point is about the half way point of the Upper Grove Walk and an ideal place for a rest, a snack or a picnic.

When you're ready to continue, go back to the main road and head east, back toward the Telescope Tree. In about 800 feet, on the left side of the road, you'll see the Wawona Tunnel Tree flat on the ground. A sign here explains that in 1881 the Yosemite Stage and Turnpike Company paid the two Scribner brothers $75 to cut an eight-foot-wide, ten-foot-high, 26-foot-long tunnel at the base of the tree so tourists could drive through it. The job took the Scribners ten days. Weighted down with tons of snow, the tree toppled over in the winter of 1969. Now its roots extend 25 feet into the air.

Cross the road, walk down the wooden steps opposite the Wawona Tunnel Tree and follow the path through more giant sequoias. In about .3 miles you'll be back at the museum.

Go around to the entrance side of the building and follow the path running into a long, wet meadow with huge sequoias growing around the edge of it. You'll cross the narrow meadow on a wooden bridge and quickly come to a fork in the trail. On your left, near the road, is the 290-foot Columbia Tree, the tallest sequoia in the grove. (On your right are the restrooms.)

This giant sequoia in the **Mariposa Grove** *(Walk No. 14) was dedicated "to the Unknown Dead of the World War" (World War I) by the American Legion in 1921.* ▶

Take the right fork, follow the path along the southeast edge of the meadow and enjoy the views of the huge sequoias on the other side of the lush grass. About 800 feet from the fork in the trail you'll pass, on your right, a sequoia fallen across the meadow. In another couple of hundred feet you'll come to the road. On the other side of the road and about 50 feet to the left is the giant Mariposa Tree, one of the most beautifully shaped sequoias in the grove.

Follow the trail on the opposite side of the road. (A sign identifies it as the "Loop Trail to Wawona.") In a few hundred feet you'll come to a level parklike area with more than a dozen giant sequoias. Take a right at the trail junction here and walk another 500 feet or so to explore this delightful grove.

Then walk back to where you saw the sequoia fallen across the meadow. Walk across this natural boardwalk to the northwest side of the meadow, go right at the trail junction and walk back toward the museum. You'll pass more sequoias and you'll enjoy the views of the giant trees on the southeast side of the meadow. Then you'll cross an arm of the meadow on a wooden bridge and, in another couple of hundred feet, reach the museum.

From there you ride the tram back to the Lower Grove. En route your driver will tell you more facts about sequoias and you'll get another look at the trees you saw on your way up.

The tram stops for a few minutes near the Grizzly Giant. Get out here and follow the smooth, wide path that winds .8 miles, mostly downhill, to the parking area. On your way you'll pass seven interesting named trees as well as a half-dozen signs describing the habits of giant sequoias.

The first major tree you'll come to is the Grizzly Giant. It's about 2,700 years old, 209 feet high and more than 27 feet wide at its base—the oldest and most massive tree in the grove. One of its limbs is more than six feet thick—wider than the trunk of most trees.

Just north of the Grizzly Giant is the California Tunnel Tree. In 1895 a seven-foot-wide, ten-foot-high tunnel was cut in its base so, when snow in the Upper Grove made the Wawona Tunnel Tree inaccessible, winter tourists could drive through this tree instead. Despite the tunnel, the tree is still alive and well.

After you've walked through the California Tunnel Tree retrace your steps to the Grizzly Giant and follow the path to the parking loop.

About halfway back you'll pass the Bachelor and the Three Graces, four sequoias that demonstrate how close to each other these giants can grow.

Then you'll cross the loop road and pass more large sequoias on your right. You'll cross the road again near the parking area and immediately pass by the roots of the Fallen Monarch, which reach 15 feet into the air. This ten-foot-thick behemoth fell at least 100 years ago (and maybe much earlier) but it shows little sign of decay.

15 Tuolumne Grove

This moderate 2.3-mile round trip takes you through the heart of the Tuolumne Grove of giant sequoias. On a .3-mile nature trail at the Walk's half-way point, eight plaques explain how the massive, cinnamon-colored giants propagate and how they're able to live as long as 3,000 years to become "the largest living organisms on the planet." On your way to the nature trail you walk through the remains of a "tunnel tree."

To reach the trailhead, get on the Big Oak Flat Road (Route 120), which links the park's Big Oak Flat Entrance with Route 140. Then turn north onto the Tioga Road, which joins the Big Oak Flat Road about ten miles west of Route 140 and about 8.5 miles east of the Big Oak Flat Entrance. In about .5 miles you'll come to the trailhead parking area, on the left.

From here you follow the Old Big Oak Flat Road as it makes a steep, curving descent into the Toulumne Grove. En route you'll pass enormous, three- to four-foot-thick evergreen trees and many dogwoods.

In about a mile the road levels off and you'll see a large sequoia on your left. This tree was the first sequoia we ever saw and we still remember our reaction: This . . . *thing,* we thought, is simply too *big* to be a tree. It's surreal. It looks like something in a

---

Wapama Falls *(Walk No. 16) plunge nearly 1,400 feet down the almost vertical walls of Hetchy Hetchy Reservoir.* ►

Disney cartoon, a fantastic treehouse where dwarfs or elves might live.

On the opposite side of the road, a .1-mile spur road goes off to the right. Follow it past two smaller sequoias and you'll quickly come to the "tunnel tree." A plaque explains that a "tunnel was cut in this dead stump" in 1878 "so tourists on the Big Oak Flat Road could ride through a tree." All that's left of the nine-foot-wide, 12-foot-high tunnel are the jagged remains of two sides of the tree, each now no more than 50 feet high.

After passing through the tunnel the spur road quickly returns to the Old Big Oak Flat Road. Beside the intersection is a split-rail fence that marks the beginning of the nature trail. A plaque here says: "The massive trees you're about to see are the largest living organisms on the planet."

As you follow the nature trail through the open, sunny grove, you're surrounded by giant sequoias and dogwoods. Eight plaques explain, among other things, how the sequoias' bark—rich in tannic acid and the "thickest . . . of any tree in the world"—helps prolong the life of the trees by protecting them from insects, fungus and fire, and how the sequoias not only tolerate forest fires but actually require them to flourish.

Dead sequoias as big as bullet trains lie beside the live trees. One of the fallen giants is the Leaning Tower Tree, which toppled in 1983. Nearly 200 feet long and 12 feet high at its base, it looks almost like a small ridge beside the trail. Its roots alone are 30 feet across.

After you've walked the nature trail, follow the Old Big Oak Flat Road back to your car.

16 Wapama Falls

This moderate five-mile round trip runs along the steep shore of the man made Hetch Hetchy Reservoir, the largest lake in the park. The Walk offers continuous views of Kolana Rock, Hetch Hetchy Dome and LeConte Point, all of which rise dramatically from the blue-green, eight-mile-long lake, as well as vistas of Tueeulala and Wapama falls, which drop hundreds of feet down the lake's bare granite cliffs.

The Walk is best taken in the spring, for two reasons. Like other cascades in the park that are fed by melting snow, Wapama Falls lose much of their volume by early summer and Tueeulala Falls dry up entirely. Also, much of the Walk is over exposed, sunny ledges, which can make for tedious tramping on warm summer days. If you have to take this Walk on a warm day, try getting an early start so you'll be walking in the cooler part of the day.

Watch out for poison oak along some sections of the trail. Its small, lobed leaves, which look like miniature oak leaves, grow in groups of three. To make sure you don't walk through it, stay on the path and try not to brush against plants along the way.

The reservoir is in the northwest part of the park. From the Big Oak Flat Entrance Station, on the west boundary of the park, you drive one mile north to the junction of Evergreen Road and Route 120, then go right on the well-named Evergreen Road, which runs through the impressive pine and fir trees of Stanislaus National Forest. In about seven miles you'll pass Evergreen Lodge, which has a restaurant and small grocery store and snack bar. In another half-mile you'll reach Camp Mather, a recreation area operated by the City of San Francisco, which also has a small grocery store and snack bar. At the three-way intersection at Camp Mather you take a right onto the Hetch Hetchy Road. In about 1.5 miles you'll reenter the park at the Hetch Hetchy Entrance Station.

The road soon begins a winding, 1,200-foot descent to the reservoir. On your way you'll have many views to your left of the steep, evergreen-festooned granite walls of the Tuolumne canyon, the 900-foot-wide O'Shaughnessy Dam across the narrow canyon and Hetch Hetchy Reservoir to the right of the dam. Almost eight miles from the entrance station you'll come to the one-way loop road that takes you, counterclockwise, to the edge of the dam. You'll pass a restroom and caretakers' housing, on the right, and you'll have your first close view of the reservoir. Tueeulala Falls, wispy and gossamer thin,

Clouds Rest (left) and Half Dome (center right) seen from **Olmsted Point** *(Walk No. 17).* ▶

flows down the rock wall of the north side of the lake. To the right of Tueeulala is the broader, fuller Wapama Falls. To the right of Wapama is the tiny Hetch Hetchy Dome and to the right of the dome, on the south side of the lake, is the near vertical prow of Kolana Rock, rising more than 1,200 feet above the lake.

Park on the loop road near the south end of the dam and walk along the top of the dam toward the north side of the lake. To your left, down the deep, narrow canyon of the Tuolumne, you can see a white column of water shooting out the bottom of the dam and creating white foam as it smashes into the canyon wall. On your right is a 180-degree view of the steep, pointed walls of Tuolumne Canyon on both sides of the lake. Plaques near the center of the dam tell you that the structure is 426 feet high and 900 feet long on its crest, where you're standing.

On the north side of the dam you'll immediately enter a truck-size 600-foot tunnel through the canyon's rock wall. When you come out the other end, you'll be on a sandy, nearly level roadbed. As you walk past manzanita bushes you'll have constant views of the lake.

The road, now paved in places, runs in and out of trees as it climbs up the western shore of the lake. In about .5 miles the road crosses a tiny stream on stones. Then it crosses a larger creek on a wooden bridge; just to the left of the trail the stream trickles off a ledge.

Now the road curves briefly away from the shore as it climbs higher and higher above the lake.

About .9 miles from the trailhead, the trail to the falls branches off the right side of the road and heads toward the lake. Kolana Rock will now be ahead of you, the dam on your right.

The trail soon curves through lush, level meadows, then switches back and forth down through a shady oak grove before emerging on a broad ledge shelf near the lake. From here you can see the long, narrow ribbon of Tueeulala Falls, Hetch Hetchy Dome, Kolana Rock and the dam astride the narrow west end of the lake.

The trail next passes a lovely natural water composition. An inch-thick, 20-foot-wide sheet of water trickles and slides down a smooth ledge on the left of the path. The water flows into a wide, shallow pool whose edge is thick with grass and wildflowers that attract dragonflies and butterflies. The water then flows out of the pool, across the path and over the ledge to the lake.

The trail now runs along a wide rock shelf at the edge of the lake. The ledge is a long, natural belvedere with continuous views up and down the reservoir. Walk slowly here and savor the ever-closer vistas of Tueeulala Falls as they splash down the 1,000-foot cliff on your left. Savor, too, the ever more dramatic views of the lake's bare, steep slopes. They now seem higher, starker, rockier. The eastern end of the lake looks almost like a fjord.

The trail passes briefly through trees before offering even better views of Tueeulala Falls and the east end of the lake.

Soon you have views of both Tueeulala and Wapama falls. Tueeulala is long and thin and blown easily to the left and right like a veil as it falls down the sheer cliff. Wapama, in contrast, is short (from this vantage point) but wide, thick and vigorous; the wind could do nothing to it if it tried.

The trail passes below Tueeulala Falls on a wooden bridge, then goes smoothly over rough talus slopes below the nearly vertical cliffs on the left. Be sure to look back for still more views of the falls.

Finally the trail switches back and forth, on cobbled stone steps, down to the base of raging Wapama Falls. Wapama plunges a total of nearly 1,400 feet down a niche in the north wall of the reservoir just to the left of Hetch Hetchy Dome. It makes two foaming leaps, which together create a long, subtle S-curve. Then the fall splits apart on the talus slope along the shore and becomes a 400-foot-wide delta of noisy, misty cascades before finally spending itself in the reservoir.

You can watch these cascades from a series of five bridges, four steel and one wooden, that span the boulders at the base of the falls. Together they create a catwalk on which you can walk over the churning white water. The bridge you reach first has the best view of the upper fall but the second offers a view of the lower fall *and* Tueeulala Falls *and another* fall, just above the bridge, that leaps 25 feet over boulders into foaming rapids beneath your feet. So violent is

Polly Dome rises from the northern shore of **Tenaya Lake** *(Walk No. 18). To the right are Medlicott and Mariuolumne domes, on the horizon, and Pywiak Dome, in front of them.* ▶

the water here in the spring that it sends mist 30 feet into the air. The wind carries the spray even farther, soaking the path and the bridges and sometimes wetting walkers, too. On warm days, the mist is delightfully refreshing.

Kolana Rock is directly on the other side of the reservoir. In the narrow eastern end of the lake, evergreen-dappled cliffs rise steeply and elegantly above dark blue waters.

The best place to picnic at the falls is just west of the first bridge. It's dry there and you can see more of the falls from that spot than from anywhere else along the catwalk.

When you're ready to return to your car, follow the trail back to the loop road.

17 Olmsted Point

This easy half-mile round trip takes you to a stunning view of the awesome bare rock landscape of upper Tenaya Creek. You'll see Tenaya Peak and Polly, Pywiack and Medlicott domes rising from the shores of Tenaya Lake, and Half Dome, Clouds Rest and Mount Watkins ascending steeply from the gray ledge floor of Tenaya Canyon.

The Walk begins at Olmsted Point, an overlook on the Tioga Road about nine miles west of the Tuolumne Meadows Visitor Center and almost two miles west of Lake Tenaya. The overlook itself offers one of the best roadside vistas in the park. To the far left is Tenaya Lake (Walk No. 18). Beyond the lake and rising more than 1,600 feet above it is the bare summit of 9,810-foot Polly Dome. On the slopes of Polly Dome are three smaller gray domes: Mountaineers, Harlequin and Stately Pleasure. To the right of the domes is the canyon of Tenaya Creek, which flows in and out of Tenaya Lake. To the right of the canyon is haystack-shaped Pywiak Dome, which rises more than 700 feet above the lake. In the notch formed by Polly Dome on the left and Pywiak Dome on the right you can see 12,590-foot Mount Conness, the sixth highest peak in the park; Conness is on the Sierra Crest, on the eastern boundary of the park. To the right of Pywiak Dome is Medlicott Dome, which is 130 feet lower than Polly Dome. Rising steeply from the east shore of Lake Tenaya are the bare rock slopes of 10,310-foot Tenaya Peak. Ahead of you are the long, incredibly flat slopes of 9,926-foot Clouds Rest and, to the right of Clouds Rest, the utterly bare rock face of 8,842-foot Half Dome.

You get an even better version of this view on the dome to the east of Olmsted Point and about 250 feet above it. To get there, follow the stone-lined path that begins on the ledge in front of the parking area, near signs explaining the nature of domes and the effect of glaciers on the Tenaya Creek drainage.

The path descends about 200 feet and crosses the trail linking Yosemite Valley with Tenaya Lake. Go straight ahead and climb up to the top of the dome. Walk past pines, junipers, manzanita and scrub oak to the east edge of the dome. You are now on the rim of Tenaya Canyon, whose gray rock walls drop 1,000 feet below you. From here you can see everything you could see from Olmsted Point, from Polly Dome on your left to Half Dome on your right, and all the way down Tenaya Canyon into Yosemite Valley. To the right of the gray rock canyon are the steep rock walls of Mount Watkins. To the left of Watkins, on the south wall of Yosemite Valley, is 7,214-foot Glacier Point (Walk No. 8).

The view is surrealistic: From the domes on your left to Mount Watkins on your right, it looks as if the entire world — or at least all the world you can see — is made mostly of rock: vast, gray, glacier-scoured granite ledge, sometimes decorated by evergreen trees and water but mostly smooth and mostly bare. Here the world seems to exist absolutely without soil — the trees seem to grow out of solid rock. Here the body of the earth has lost almost all its flesh of plants and trees and is left with only the skeleton of its rock.

After you've enjoyed this remarkable vista, follow the path back to your car.

18 Tenaya Lake

This easy three-mile round trip takes you

Snow-flecked Mount Dana (left) and Mount Gibbs rise in the distance beyond **Dog Lake** *(Walk No. 21).* ▶

along the southeastern shore of mile-long Tenaya Lake. Along the way you'll have often continuous views, across the lake, of bare rock landmarks, including Tenaya Peak, Mount Hoffmann, Pywiak and Polly domes and the knobs on Polly Dome known as Harlequin, Mountaineers and Stately Pleasure domes.

The Walk begins in a parking area on the east side of the Tioga Road, near the southwestern end of Tenaya Lake, about 1.5 miles northeast of Olmsted Point (Walk No. 17) and about seven miles southwest of the Tuolumne Meadows Visitor Center. The paved parking area, which is also where the Walk to the Sunrise High Sierra Camp (No. 27) begins, is marked by a brown-and-white park sign saying "Sunrise."

The trail begins at a gated road at the eastern end of the parking area. Follow the level road until you come to Tenaya Creek, the outlet of Tenaya Lake, in just a few hundred feet. The wide creek is usually shallow enough so you can cross it on stones. Sometimes, however (especially in early summer or after rainstorms), it's several feet high and you have to wade across. The creek is barely moving and its bottom is smooth so wading isn't difficult. Take off your boots and socks and anything else you don't want to get wet and bring along a small towel to dry off with on the other side of the creek.

On the far side of the creek the trail heads to the right. But instead of following that path now, go straight ahead through the pine trees. In less than

100 feet you'll reach the sandy shore of Tenaya Lake. Rising above the Tioga Road on the far side of the lake, is the steep, nearly bare rock of Stately Pleasure Dome, a part of Polly Dome. To the right of the dome is the narrow canyon of Tenaya Creek. On the right side of the canyon is the much smaller Pywiak Dome. On the right side of the lake are the slopes of Tenaya Peak. From here the world appears to be a very simple place, one made only of blue-green water and sweeping gray rock decorated with evergreens.

Now go back to the trail (by the creek) and follow the unusually smooth path to the left. The trail briefly follows the creek downstream and then runs through scrub pines. A lush meadow extends for several hundred feet on your right.

In just a few hundred feet the trail splits. The right fork goes to Sunrise High Sierra Camp. The left fork goes along the lake.

Take a left. The path curves along a row of large granite stones and quickly brings you close to the lake. For the rest of the Walk the path is seldom more than 30 feet from the shore.

For the next .2 miles or so there are no trees on the left of the trail so you have continuous open views of the Sierra rock sculpture across the lake. The panorama includes the broad, gray hulk of 10,850-foot Mount Hoffmann, in the very center of the park. Note the rampartlike rocks and chimneylike outcrop on its summit. To the right of Hoffmann is the knob of 10,845-foot Tuolumne Peak. Farther to the right, on the north shore, is Stately Pleasure Dome, whose steep slopes rise directly out of the aqua-colored water. Behind Stately Pleasure Dome are Harlequin and Mountaineers domes. All three are part of 9,810-foot Polly Dome. To the right of Polly Dome is Tenaya Canyon, and to the right of the canyon is smooth, sugarloaf-shaped Pywiak Dome. The steep, flat two-mile-wide slopes of 10,301-foot Tenaya Peak are to the right of the trail, on the southeast side of the lake.

You'll keep seeing this view, through the sparse pines and other evergreens, as you walk along the lake. You'll also pass pretty patches of Labrador tea and heather and you'll hear the pleasant slapping of waves against the rocky shore.

As you approach the beach on the northeastern side of the lake, the slopes of Polly Dome become more distinct. Look carefully and you may spot climbers on the sheer rock walls.

After crossing several trickling streamlets you'll reach the quarter-mile-long beach at the end of the lake. From here you'll have another panoramic view across the lake that includes Tenaya Peak, now on your left; Mount Hoffmann, ahead, and Stately Pleasure Dome, now on your right.

The views get better as you walk along the soft, sandy beach, toward Stately Pleasure Dome. However, you quickly come to Tenaya Creek, which flows into the lake near the southeastern end of the beach. Tenaya is the same creek you crossed at the beginning of the Walk (where it flowed *out* of the lake) and, of course, the same creek you'll have to cross again on your way back to your car. If you had to wade across the creek there, you'll probably have to wade across it here and, of course, to wade across it twice more on your return trip. If you think four wet stream crossings on one Walk is a bit much, turn around here and follow the path back to your car. If you don't mind wading, or if the creek is shallow, then by all means walk across and stroll along the rest of the beach before you turn around. Whatever you do, you'll get a second look at the views, and from another perspective, as you walk back to the trailhead.

The beach, by the way, is a beautiful, sunny swimming spot—if you don't mind cold water.

19 May Lake

This moderate 3.4-mile round trip takes you up the slopes of Mount Hoffmann to the shores of beautiful May Lake. You'll enjoy panoramic views that include the Sierra Crest, the Cathedral Range, the Clark Range, Clouds Rest, Half Dome and the Tenaya Lake basin.

The paved road to the trailhead begins on the north side of the Tioga Road, about 2.3 miles west of Olmsted Point (Walk No. 17) and about 11 miles west of the Tuolumne Meadows Visitor Center. A brown-and-white sign near the intersection says "May Lake." The road climbs through a forest of rocks and scrub pines, then becomes more level before dead-ending at a parking area beside a tiny pond about 1.8 miles from the Tioga Road. The well-worn 1.2-mile trail to May Lake begins here.

Cross the culvert at the southern end of the 100-foot-long pond and follow the wide, sandy trail through evergreen woods. The trail soon runs over ledge, then through trees again, then over more ledge as it climbs gently up the slope of Mount Hoffmann. After about .5 miles you start to glimpse the sharp-pointed peaks of the Cathedral Range and the snow-topped Clark Range through the trees, behind you and on your right. The views get better with every step and, as the trail switches back and forth over open, rocky ledges, you start to see Half Dome, at the eastern end of Yosemite Valley. Then the trail levels off and enters the open pine and hemlock woods that rim the east shore of 9,320-foot-high May Lake.

In a few hundred feet you'll reach a trail junction. The right fork will quickly bring you to the white tents of the May Lake High Sierra Camp. When the camp is open (from early July to early September) you can get water here and buy candy bars and other snacks at the camp store. On the opposite shore of the round, quarter-mile-wide lake, the rough, nearly bare ledges of Mount Hoffmann rise straight out of the blue water. Foot-thick slices of tree trunks, placed along the shore, make fine seats from which to enjoy the vista.

When you're ready to continue, follow the pleasant path that, as you face the lake, runs to the right (north) along the lakeshore. The trail soon runs gently up through a sunny woodland, away from the lake, and then through a small linear meadow. A stream meanders through the meadow, on your right, and a picturesque cliff rises on your left.

Then the trail leaves the meadow and, less than .5 miles from May Lake, descends gently but quickly to a low ledge on the right side of the path. The view from here is even better than the one on your way to May Lake. On your far left are the slopes of Mount Hoffmann and 10,845-foot Tuolumne Peak. To the east and northeast, in the distance, are the snow-capped peaks of the Sierra Crest, including, from left to right, 12,590-foot Mount Conness, 13,053-foot Mount Dana and 12,764-foot Mount Gibbs. Four miles to the east, and to the right of Mount Gibbs, are 10,940-foot-high Cathedral Peak, Unicorn Peak and other bare, pointed summits of the Cathedral Range. On your right and fifteen miles to the south are the snowy peaks of the Clark Range. Far to the right and only six miles away is the long, bare, flat slope of Tenaya Canyon and the 9,926-foot summit of Clouds Rest. Below you is the evergreen-festooned rock world of the Tenaya Lake basin. Tiny Raisin Lake is less than three-quarters of a mile away. Tenaya Lake is two miles away. Rising on the opposite side of Tenaya Lake, to the right of Cathedral Peak, is 10,301-foot Tenaya Peak. Left of Tenaya Lake is Polly Dome.

Take time to savor this rich panorama and, when you're ready, retrace your steps to your car.

If you have some extra time on your way back to the parking area, you may want to explore the area around May Lake and the High Sierra Camp. Be sure, however, to stay on established trails and take care not to harm delicate vegetation.

20 Tuolumne Meadows

This easy, level, mile-long round trip takes you through the heart of Tuolumne Meadows, the largest subalpine meadow in the Sierra Nevada. As you cross the nearly flat, three-mile-long grassland you'll have views of bare rock promontories rising in every direction: Mount Dana, Mount Gibbs and the Kuna Crest; Daff, Fairview, Lembert and Pothole domes; and Cathedral, Echo, Unicorn, Johnson, Mammoth and Ragged peaks. You'll also see the effervescent Soda Springs and the interesting exhibit about Tuolumne Meadows in the historic Parsons Memorial Lodge.

The Walk begins beside a painted crosswalk on the Tioga Road, about .1 miles east of the Tuolumne Meadows Visitor Center. Park on the side of the road closest to the meadow. Then look for the wide, sandy trail and a steel sign that says that the Soda Springs are .5 miles away.

Start following the level path across the wide meadow and you'll immediately see bare rock promontories rising above the evergreen-bordered fields. Ahead on the horizon is the long, bare ridge of

---

The spires of Cathedral Peak rise more than 1,600 feet above **Lower Cathedral Lake** *(Walks No. 22 and 27).* ▶

10,912-foot Ragged Peak. To your right, less than a mile away, the smooth, steep 9,450-foot Lembert Dome (Walk No. 21) rises almost 900 feet above the meadow. To the right of the dome, on the snowy Sierra Crest, is 13,053-foot Mount Dana, the second highest peak in the park. On your left is Pothole Dome, which rises more than 200 feet above the meadow. Behind Pothole Dome and rising more than 300 feet above it is Daff Dome. Left of Pothole Dome, on the south side of the Tioga Road, is Fairview Dome, almost 300 feet higher than Lembert.

As you walk across the meadow you'll see more peaks to the right of Mount Dana, including, from left to right: 12,764-foot Mount Gibbs, the fifth highest peak in the park, on the Sierra Crest; 12,117-foot Mammoth Peak and the long steep Kuna Crest. Behind you you'll see more and more of the delicately pointed, nearly 11,000-foot-high peaks of the Cathedral Range. First you'll see Unicorn Peak on the left and Cathedral Peak on the right. Then you'll see the Echo Peaks; the Cockscomb, behind them, and 11,070-foot Johnson Peak to the left.

As you traverse the meadow the blue Tuolumne River will twinkle in the sunshine as it meanders on your left. You'll also see Belding ground squirrels, which hold their paws in front of them like prairie dogs when they sit up. In July the meadows will be thick with wildflowers.

In about .4 miles you'll come to the stout wooden bridge over the Tuolumne. Its foot-thick timber rails make nice benches on which to sit and enjoy the views of the natural rock sculpture to the south, west and east, and to watch and listen to the shallow river burbling softly over its stony bottom.

Cross the bridge, take a left and enjoy more views of the Tuolumne as you briefly follow the wide trail downstream.

In about 100 feet you'll come to a trail junction. Take the path to the right, which quickly takes you up a grassy slope to Parsons Memorial Lodge, a handsome fieldstone structure built in 1915 by the Sierra Club and named in honor of Edward Taylor Parsons, a former director. The building is usually open two or three afternoons a week in the summer — up-to-date information on days and times is available at park visitor centers — and the large one-room building contains an attractive exhibit on the history of Tuolumne Meadows. The displays note that John Muir herded sheep here in the 1860s and later wrote that the meadows are "the most delightful summer pleasure park in all the high Sierra." Muir called the meadows "charming sauntering grounds from which the glorious mountains may be enjoyed as they look down in divine serenity over the majestic swaths of forests that clothe their bases."

Just west of the lodge is the one-room McCauley Cabin, built in 1898 by the McCauley brothers, who raised cattle here in the early 1900s. (The log cabin is now a ranger residence, so you can't go inside.)

On the grassy slope to the east of the lodge, about halfway between it and the bridge over the Tuolumne River, are the Soda Springs. Signs beside the wood enclosure around the bubbling springs note that the naturally carbonated waters — which, not surprisingly, taste like mineral water—"have refreshed wilderness travelers for centuries" and that the Sierra Club, "under the leadership of John Muir, began its Annual Outings" from this "idyllic spot."

When you're ready to return to your car, follow the path from the springs down to the bridge (which you can see from the springs), retrace your route across the meadow and enjoy the mountains and domes all around you from a different direction.

21 Lembert Dome & Dog Lake

This moderate four-mile excursion takes you to the top of 9,450-foot Lembert Dome, where you have bird's-eye views of Tuolumne Meadows and panoramic vistas of the Cathedral Range and the Sierra Crest, and to pretty Dog Lake, which offers even more views of mountains.

You can approach Lembert Dome and Dog Lake from the west or the east. The western trail is rough and steep. The eastern trail, however, is smooth and

Cathedral Peak rises nearly 1,400 feet above **Upper Cathedral Lake** *(Walks No. 22 and 27).* ▶

well graded. To reach it, take the paved road to Tuolumne Lodge, which begins on the south side of the Tioga Road about 1.5 miles east of the Tuolumne Meadows Visitor Center. A sign at the intersection says, among other things, "Tuolumne HSC" (for "High Sierra Camp"). The road heads east, parallel to the Tioga Road. In about .4 miles you'll come to a parking area on your left marked by a sign saying "Dog Lake" and "John Muir [Trail]." The trail to Lembert Dome and Dog Lake begins at the north end of the parking area. There's no sign by the trailhead—just look for the path that leads up the slope toward the Tioga Road (and toward the sound of traffic).

In less than .1 mile you'll cross the road and climb up stone steps into the pleasant, grassy lodgepole forest on the other side of the highway. The trail switches gently back and forth as it climbs up a steep slope.

Soon you'll see mountains through the trees. To the east is Mammoth Peak. To the south, more than six miles away, are the usually snowy summits of the Cathedral Range, including, from left to right, Amelia Earhart, Parsons, Fletcher and Vogelsang peaks, all more than 11,000 feet high. Johnson Peak is just three miles to the south and Cathedral and Unicorn peaks are in the southwest.

After climbing about 300 feet in just a quarter-mile, the trail levels off and soon comes to a junction. The left fork goes to Lembert Dome, the right one to Dog Lake.

Take the trail to the left, which climbs gently, then a bit more steeply to the low pass, or saddle, between Lembert Dome and Dog Dome. As you approach the saddle you'll see the long light gray rock ridge of Dog Dome on your right.

When you reach the highest point of the saddle, climb up Lembert Dome, on your left. The top of Lembert is a steep-sided .3-mile ridge that runs from the northeast (at the saddle) to the southwest. The crest of the dome has no path. Just pick your route as you climb to the summit, near the midpoint of the dome, and as you explore the dome from one end to the other, savoring the continuous and ever-changing views in every direction. Indeed, the top of Lembert Dome is a short, glorious walk all by itself. Spend at least an hour here sampling the vistas.

Toward the southern end of the ridge, for example, you have bird's-eye views of Tuolumne Meadows — Kitty and Puppy domes to the south; the Soda Springs and Parsons Memorial Lodge to the west and Pothole and Daff domes beyond; the Tuolumne River meandering placidly through the broad meadow. Mountains are all around you: Dana, Gibbs and Mammoth Peak to the east, Ragged Peak to the north, more of the Sierra Crest to the northeast, Mount Hoffmann and Tuolumne Peak to the west, Cathedral and Unicorn peaks to the south, and the massive snow-flecked peaks of the Cathedral Range to the southeast. The contrasts among the smooth, light-green meadows, the dark, pointed lodgepole pines, and the rough gray peaks are striking.

When you're ready to continue, go back to the saddle between Lembert and Dog domes and follow

the path to the right, back to the trail junction. Go left at the intersection and follow the nearly level trail through the evergreen forest beneath the nearly vertical north slope of Dog Dome, which will be on your left. You'll soon pass a 200-foot-long, 100-foot-wide pond below the dome.

About .5 miles from the trail junction you'll reach another intersection. Follow the trail to the right as it climbs gently up a ridge.

After about .1 miles the path levels off and you'll come to still another junction. Take a right again and, in about .2 miles, you'll reach the southwestern shore of Dog Lake.

The lake is about .2 miles wide at its widest point and almost .5 miles long — one of the largest in the area. It's also one of the prettiest, fringed with grass and clusters of lodgepole pines and surrounded by bare mountain peaks.

You can see the mountains from a smooth, nearly level path winding around the lake. If you follow the trail clockwise, in less than .1 miles you'll come to a sandy point on the northwest shore that's perfect for a rest or a picnic. To the east, across the lake, you'll see Mount Dana, Mount Gibbs and Mammoth Peak. To the south you'll see the tops of Unicorn and Cathedral Peaks. If you walk counterclockwise along the southern shore you'll have views of the long, bare ridge of 10,912-foot Ragged Peak, to the

---

Mount Gibbs is reflected in a pond on the south side of the Tioga Road, about 1.6 miles from the trail to the **Gaylor Lakes** *(Walk No. 23).*
◀

north.

After you've enjoyed the views, follow the trail back to your car.

22 Cathedral Lakes

This moderate seven-mile round trip takes you to the mountain-ringed Cathedral Lakes. En route you'll have close views of Fairview, Mariuolumne and Medlicott domes; Cathedral, Echo and Unicorn peaks; the Cockscomb and the slopes of Tresidder Peak. From the outlet of Lower Cathedral Lake, you'll also have a sweeping view of the Tenaya Lake basin and the monumental rock sculpture around it, including Mount Hoffmann, Tuolumne and Tenaya peaks and Pywiak and Polly domes.

The Walk begins in the southwest corner of the Cathedral Lakes trailhead parking area, which is on the south side of the Tioga Road, about .5 miles west of the Tuolumne Meadows Visitor Center.

The trail crosses a sandy, rocky, lodgepole pine forest as it heads southwest, away from the meadows. Just .1 miles from the parking area the trail crosses another trail, then climbs, mostly gently but sometimes earnestly, up the evergreen-forested slope. As you climb you'll have occasional views, through the trees behind you, of Tuolumne Meadows, the Tuolumne River meandering through it and, from left to right, Ragged Peak to the north and Mount Dana, Mount Gibbs and Mammoth Peak to the east.

The trail levels off after about .7 miles and, for almost a mile, crosses gently rolling woodlands. Along the way you'll have glimpses, through the trees, of Unicorn Peak and 10,940-foot Cathedral Peak, on your left, and 9,731-foot Fairview Dome, on your right.

The trail then crosses a small meadow and several tiny streams before it comes to within 300 feet of the bare north slope of Cathedral Peak. The peak rises suddenly, almost surrealistically, from the forest as a massive, irregular pyramid of smooth light gray granite.

As the trail curves around the west side of the peak, you'll see its pointed summit on your left. On your right you'll have another view of the smooth, bare, steep-sided Fairview Dome, which looks like a giant boulder dropped in the middle of the lodge-pole forest.

Then the trail crosses a branch of Cathedral Creek and switches back and forth as it climbs an evergreen slope. Through the trees you'll have more views of Fairview Dome and glimpses of Medlicott and Mariuolumne domes and the Tenaya Lake basin to your right.

After a quarter-mile or so the trail levels off. Then it passes through dry, sandy woods, descends gently through a rocky area and, about three miles from the trailhead, reaches a trail junction. Here, on your left, the pointed spires of the summit of Cathedral Peak tower almost 1,500 feet above you.

Follow the path to the right, which leads to Lower Cathedral Lake. The trail crosses several tiny streams as it winds down a rocky slope. Then it crosses a small meadow, goes over a low ridge and then cuts across a large meadow laced with meandering streams and bordered by mountains. Finally, you climb up on the long, low granite ledge in front of you and suddenly you see Lower Cathedral Lake.

You are now in the middle of one of the best lake-and-mountain compositions in the Sierra. The dark-blue, .5-mile-long lake rests like a jewel in a dramatic natural setting. The lake is bordered by the smooth ledge you're standing on, by the wide meadows you just crossed—whose flatness echoes the lake's—and by the curving wall of mountains that wraps around the entire scene. Cathedral Peak is to the east. The lower slopes of the massif of Tresidder Peak are to the south. Ahead of you, beyond the outlet at the western end of the lake, are Mount Hoffmann and Tuolumne Peak. To the north are Medlicott and Mariuolumne domes.

Follow the well-worn path to your left along the undulating shore. You'll walk under pines, past heather and Labrador tea, and close to the lapping waves of the lake.

Soon you'll reach the western end of the tarn. Here its outlet flows over the ledge beneath your feet, drops in a three-foot waterfall, then slides down

Summer snow around a pond in Dana Meadows, opposite the trail to the **Gaylor Lakes** *(Walk No. 23). Mammoth Peak is in the background.* ▶

the steep, half-mile-long rock slope toward Tenaya Creek. Below you lie Tenaya Lake and the ever-green-dotted rock basin around it. To the right of Tenaya Lake are, from left to right, Stately Pleasure, Harlequin and Mountaineers domes, all part of the much larger Polly Dome. You can also see the Tioga Road between the domes and the lake, as well as the tall, thin, smooth-polished Pywiak Dome on the south side of the road. Mount Hoffmann and Tuolumne Peak are ahead on the horizon. Tenaya Peak is on your left. Medlicott and Mariuolumne domes are on your right. Look behind you and you'll see the vast rock amphitheater curving around the eastern and southern shores of Lower Cathedral Lake. Cathedral Peak is on the left, the Echo Peaks are to the right of Cathedral Peak and the lower slopes of the massif of Tresidder Peak parallel the south shore.

Cross the outlet and keep following the path around the lake. You'll pass campsites on the north shore and enjoy the changing shapes of Cathedral Peak as you see it from different perspectives. On your right, a flank of Tresidder Peak looks like one wall of a square castle; the top of that castellated wall rises from left to right.

You'll soon reach the long, low rock ridge on the east side of the lake. Cross the inlet of the lake where it slides elegantly over a low place on the ridge in thin, wide sheets of placid water and follow the inlet over the flat, smooth ledge until you rejoin the path that runs across the meadow.

When you're ready to leave the lake, retrace your route across the meadow and enjoy the changing views of Cathedral Peak and especially the Eichorn Pinnacle on its left summit. Then climb back up to the trail junction .5 miles from the lake.

Now take a right and follow the path as it gently climbs through sunny, open evergreen woods to Upper Cathedral Lake. You'll have close views of Cathedral Peak, now less than half a mile away, on your left. At one point, one summit of the peak looks boldly symmetrical, like a pyramid.

About .6 miles from the junction you reach the upper lake. The 600-foot-wide tarn is ringed by meadows and its gracefully undulating shore is set with smooth, low ledges that are perfect for picnicking and lounging. The grassy basin is ringed on three sides by steep, bare mountain walls. To the northeast, the twin towers of Cathedral Peak—the Eichorn Pinnacle on the left, the clusters of spires on the right—sweep more than 1,000 feet above the lake. To the southeast are the Echo Peaks. Cathedral Peak and the Echo Peaks are linked by a long graceful saddle, which curves along the top of a glacier-carved bowl. South of the lake the slope of Tresidder Peak looks like a long, straight castellated ruin.

When you're ready to return to Tuolumne Meadows, follow the trail back to your car.

23 Gaylor Lakes

This moderately strenuous four-mile round trip takes you up the slope above Tioga Pass to

the shores of the Gaylor Lakes, to the ruins of the Great Sierra Mine, on the Sierra Crest, and to the most extensive and impressive collection of mountain views of any Great Walk in the park. From two-mile-high vantage points you'll have close views of Mount Dana, Mount Gibbs and Gaylor, Mammoth and Tioga peaks. You'll also see landmarks of the Cathedral Range—Cathedral, Fletcher, Johnson, Rafferty, Vogelsang and Unicorn peaks, the Cockscomb and Matthes Crest—as well as Tuolumne Peak, Mount Hoffmann and Lembert, Fairview and other domes in and around Tuolumne Meadows.

The Walk begins in a paved parking area on the west side of the Tioga Road, just a few feet south of the park entrance at Tioga Pass.

The trail curves through a sunny, grassy lodgepole forest as it climbs the steep slope above the pass. One by one the mountains on the opposite side of the pass come into view. First you'll see the three-mile-wide, 13,053-foot-high hulk of Mount Dana, the park's second highest peak; then, to the right of Dana, the many-pointed ridge of the snow-capped Kuna Crest; then, to the right of the Kuna Crest, the gray pyramid of the well-named 12,117-foot Mammoth Peak; and, finally, the red-tinted slopes

The Cathedral Range beyond **Middle Gaylor Lake** *(Walk No. 23).*
◀

of 12,764-foot Mount Gibbs, the park's fifth highest peak, just to the right of Dana.

The trail climbs at the rate of about 1,200 feet per mile—more steeply than any other Great Walk in Yosemite. But the climb is brief—about .5 miles— and the magnificent uninterrupted views make the work worthwhile. If you walk slowly and stop often, the climb will be easier and you'll enjoy the views longer. If you're short of time, a hike just up this slope—a one-mile round trip—would be a Great Walk all by itself.

The views get better as you climb. You'll see more and more of the broad, multipeaked massif of Dana, whose lower slopes are just a mile away. Then, below you, you'll see the tiny, emerald-green ponds in the broad Dana Meadows.

As the trail switches back and forth up the ridge, the trees thin out and your views become continuous. You'll see 11,513-foot Tioga Peak, to your right. Then, to the left of Tioga, you'll see Gaylor Peak, whose 11,004-foot summit is just .5 miles to the north, on the very ridge you're climbing.

The trail finally becomes gentler as it approaches the top of the wide, unusually smooth gravelly saddle, or low point, of the ridge. Behind you is an open 180-degree vista of bare rock massifs. From left to right the panorama includes Gaylor, whose summit is only a few hundred feet higher than you are; Tioga Peak, Mount Dana, Mount Gibbs, the Kuna Crest and Mammoth Peak—a composition of sweeping evergreen-clad slopes, graceful bare rock shoulders and imposing bare, pointed, snow-flecked summits. Six hundred feet below you, the dozens of ponds in the greensward of Dana Meadows are so far away that they look like puddles in a golf course.

As you start climbing down the other side of the ridge, another panorama opens up. Straight ahead is a bird's-eye view of Middle Gaylor Lake and the stony meadows around it. Lower Gaylor Lake is to the left. Also on your left is a long, wide view across Tuolumne Meadows to the Cathedral Range. The vista includes, from left to right, Matthes Crest, the Cockscomb, and Unicorn and Cathedral peaks in the Cathedral Range; Lembert and Fairview domes in Toulumne Meadows, Mount Hoffmann and Tuolumne Peak. Straight ahead, in the distance, are more peaks on the Sierra Crest.

As you climb down to the middle lake, the vista widens as, one by one, more peaks enter on your left. Soon, to the left of Matthes Crest, you can see, from right to left, Johnson and Rafferty peaks, the Choochoo, and Fletcher and Vogelsang peaks.

After switching back and forth down to the shore of the middle lake, the trail turns right and curves around the northern edge of the .4-mile-long tarn, often just inches from the water. From the north shore, the lake appears to rest on the very edge of the world. The only thing you see on the southern shore of the tarn is a long, low, flat ridge of grass and rocks that stretches across the rim of the lake like a dam, and the only things beyond the "dam" are the tops of the peaks of the Cathedral Range, more than seven miles away. It looks as if the lake is filling a hollow in a shelf on the rim of a huge canyon and only the low "dam" prevents the entire lake from washing down the canyon walls.

Soon you'll come to a creek flowing into the northwest corner of the lake. Cross the inlet on stones and follow the path along the burbling streamlet as the trail gently climbs up the stony meadow to Upper Gaylor Lake. The rock-coated slope of Gaylor Peak will be on your right, the bare incline of the Sierra Crest on your left. And with every step the view of mountains expands behind you. First you see only the Cathedral peaks that you saw from the middle lake. But soon you can see over the ridge on the east side of the lake—the one you just climbed over—and Mammoth Peak and the Kuna Crest come into view. Then, to the right of Mammoth Peak, you'll see Fletcher, Vogelsang and Amelia Earhart peaks, as well as 13,114-foot Mount Lyell, the park's highest peak; 12,960-foot Mount Maclure, the third highest peak, and other, lower summits of the southern Cathedral Range. Finally, the panorama widens to include Mount Hoffmann and Tuolumne Peak, to the right of the Cathedral Range.

About 1.5 miles from the trailhead you'll reach the rocky southern shore of Upper Gaylor Lake. Tioga Peak looms ahead and you'll see Mount Dana on your right, just to the left of Gaylor Peak.

You'll see more and more of Dana as you follow the path along the western shore of the 800-foot-long lake. You'll also see the ruins of a stone cabin near

10,823-foot Unicorn Peak, left, and the Cockscomb, center, south of Tuolumne Meadows, seen from the trail to **Glen Aulin High Sierra Camp** *(Walk No. 26).* ▶

the top of Tioga Hill, on your left. As you approach the northern end of the lake, you'll come to a path that follows a creek up the hill to the cabin and the remains of the Great Sierra Mine.

As you follow the steep but short (.2-mile) trail, go slowly; you'll make the climb easier and you'll have more time to appreciate the views behind you. As you rise above the upper lake you'll note that the rockbound pond fills, almost to overflowing, a saucer of land in a saddle of the Sierra Crest and that the bare land on both sides of the lake drops off sharply to the north and south. You'll also see even more of Mount Dana, as well as Mount Gibbs and Middle Gaylor Lake.

When you reach the old abandoned cabin, you'll see that its wooden roof has collapsed but that most of its well-made, three-foot-thick stone walls are still standing. Take a minute to admire the vista through what was once the cabin's southern window.

Continue a few feet more to the bare, rocky summit of Tioga Hill and you'll see a half-dozen more ruined stone structures—though none as impressive as the cabin—and the remains of a mine shaft (be careful as you walk around the edge). You'll also see Tioga and Lee Vining peaks ahead of you, to the northeast.

The trail becomes faint here but if you walk just a few hundred feet more to the northeast you'll see another mine shaft as well as small tarns on the east side of the Sierra Crest.

Now walk back to the stone cabin and climb up to the tiny knob beside it. Here you'll be 10,800 feet high—the highest point on any Great Walk in

Yosemite—and you'll enjoy one of the widest views in the park. It includes bird's-eye views of Middle Gaylor Lake, almost 500 feet below, and Upper Gaylor Lake, almost 300 feet below, and a 180-degree mountain view that ranges all the way from Tioga Peak on the left to Mount Hoffmann on the right.

After you enjoy this vista, turn around and relish the extraordinary views again on your way back to your car. As you descend the steep slope above Tioga Pass you'll have a special treat: the chance to walk "into" the stunning views that were behind you on your way up the ridge.

24 Bennettville

This undemanding three-mile round trip takes you along the four tiny Thimble Lakes to an abandoned mine tunnel and the remains of a 19th-century mining town. En route you'll have views of Mount Dana and Mount Conness, Shell and Tioga lakes, Tioga and Lee Vining peaks and other summits of the Sierra Crest.

The Walk is actually not in the park but just outside it, in the Inyo National Forest. The trail begins on the west side of Route 120, .9 miles north of the park entrance at Tioga Pass. The trailhead is marked by a brown-stained sign with yellow-painted letters. Beside the sign is an old steam engine that was once used at Bennettville.

Park by the sign and follow the old road (the remains of the old Tioga Road) to the north, parallel to Route 120. You'll quickly come to, and walk around, a large stump in the middle of the road.

About 400 feet from the trailhead you'll reach a junction. Follow the road to the left through evergreens. As the wide trail almost imperceptibly ascends the grassy slope you'll have views of .5-mile-long Tioga Lake and 13,053-foot Mount Dana, on your right, and 11,513-foot Tioga Peak straight ahead. Just to the right of and behind Tioga Peak is 11,691-foot Lee Vining Peak.

About .5 miles from the trailhead, the old road levels off in a meadow and you'll pass the first lake, a tiny, shallow 50-foot-long tarn on your right.

Just 100 feet farther is the second lake, a crescent-shaped pool, 200 feet from end to end, on the very edge of a shelf at the top of the slope above Tioga Lake. If the lake were just a few inches higher, it would spill over the brow of the hill, like water running over a dam, and pour down the hillside in a broad sheet. From the shores of this lake you can see not only Mount Dana and Tioga Peak (the latter through the trees) but also, to the right of Dana, the long, bare, many-pointed Kuna Crest. Walk out onto the ledgy knob between the two arms of the lakelet and you'll see Tioga Lake.

Follow the grassy road another .1 miles and you'll

Tuolumne Falls roars over ledges in the Tuolumne River near the **Glen Aulin High Sierra Camp** *(Walk No. 26).* ▶

reach the third lake, a 150-foot-wide, 200-foot-long tarn surrounded by grassy shores and shaded by willows and evergreens. As you walk along the western shore of the lake you'll see Tioga Peak in the distance.

Walk just a few yards more and you'll reach the fourth lake, which is separated from the third only by a 50-foot neck of land. The dark, green-black pond, easily the largest in the chain, is about 150 feet wide and almost 300 feet long.

The road now climbs gently to the top of a rise — you'll have another view of Tioga Peak here — then descends briefly toward the meadow around Mine Creek.

The route soon becomes a stony trail as it climbs to the entrance of an abandoned mine tunnel, on the left. The nine-foot-wide, seven-foot-high tunnel goes a third of a mile into the Sierra Crest. The tunnel was built in the 1880s by the Great Sierra Consolidated Silver Company, whose owners thought it would lead them to a rich vein of silver called the Sheepherder Lode. Alas, no silver was found and the mine was abandoned.

Don't go in the tunnel. It's not safe. Instead, take a look at the collection of old mining equipment on the enormous terrace of many-colored tailings in front of the tunnel and enjoy the wide view. In the meadow below are the braids of Mine Creek. On the slope on the other side of the meadow are two weathered wooden buildings — all that remains of the mining town of Bennettville, which was deserted after the mine was abandoned. Ahead, in the distance, is the dark gray-green hulk of Tioga Peak.

On your left are the often snowy peaks of the Sierra Crest. On your right is Mount Dana. Between Mount Dana and Tioga Peak is the deep, narrow canyon of Lee Vining Creek.

Keep following the rocky path beyond the entrance to the mine and down to Mine Creek. Cross the creek on stones and follow it upstream until, in a few hundred feet, you come to a small rise. From here you can see mountains in all directions. Ahead of you is the narrow, quarter-mile-long Shell Lake. Above the lake are the rough, bare slopes of the Sierra Crest. On your right is Tioga Peak. On your left is the abandoned mine. Behind you is Mount Dana.

Go back downstream and pick up the path where you crossed Mine Creek. If you continue on the path, through the evergreens, you'll quickly reach the two remaining buildings of Bennettville. One of these plain, simple structures was an assay office, the other a barn. The Forest Service began restoring the buildings in 1990 and plans to install displays that illustrate and explain the history of the site.

When you're ready to return to your car, follow the trail back to Route 120. The views of Mount Dana should be even more enjoyable on your return trip because you'll be walking "into" them.

25 Tioga Tarns

This quarter-mile loop is an easy stroll past

five tiny mountain lakes, across which you'll have views of Mount Dana and Gaylor, Mammoth and Tioga peaks.

Like the trail to Bennettville (Walk No. 24), this Walk begins on the west side of Route 120, just north of the park entrance at Tioga Pass, in the Inyo National Forest. The trailhead parking area is 1.6 miles from the park entrance and marked by a brown-stained sign with yellow-painted letters. Another sign, at the trailhead, indicates that the clockwise path begins by heading south, toward the park and parallel to Route 120. Smaller signs along the trail describe the heather, whitebark pine and other species growing at this 9,700-foot elevation. The signs also explain how the tarns were created by glaciers and how, one day, they will disappear.

You barely start walking before you see the first tarn on your left, beside the road. Across the 150-foot-long, 100-foot-wide pond you can see 11,004-foot Gaylor Peak ahead of you, 12,117-foot Mammoth Peak to the left of Gaylor and the massive 13,053-foot Mount Dana, on your far left.

The path curves to the right and, only about 50 feet from the first tarn, you'll pass the second one, on the left of the trail. Barely 10 feet wide and 30 feet long and very shallow, it's easily the smallest of the little lakes and it'll almost certainly be the first to fill up with sediments and disappear.

The White Cascade plunges into a lake-size pool beside the **Glen Aulin High Sierra Camp** *(Walk No. 26).* ►

In another 150 feet or so you'll come, on your right, to the biggest and most beautiful tarn, a placid, 150-foot-wide, 300-foot-long sheet of water ringed by grass, red heather and whitebark pines. Ahead of you, on the other side of the tarn, is the (usually) snow-flecked massif of Dana. To your left, on the north side of the lake, is the bare rock hulk of 11,513-foot Tioga Peak. On your right is Gaylor Peak. Both the view and the sunny, grassy banks of this pond invite lingering.

When you're ready to continue, follow the path through the trees to the northern end of the pond. Here, about 60 feet off the trail, to your left, is the fourth tarn, a grass-banked, 50-by-70-foot lakelet. Above the tarn you can see Tioga Peak.

Now follow the trail around the east shore of the largest tarn. You'll see Gaylor Peak on your right and there are benches along the lake in case you want to tarry and enjoy the view.

The path curves along a tiny bay near the outlet of the lake, then heads back toward the road and quickly comes to the fifth tarn, which is near the road and on your left. The path runs along the shore of this 60-by-100-foot lakelet, then immediately returns to the parking area.

26 Glen Aulin High Sierra Camp

This moderate three-day excursion takes

you to the most impressive collection of water-falls in the park. On the first day, as you follow the Tuolumne River 5.2 miles downstream from Tuolumne Meadows, you'll pass Tuolumne Falls and literally hundreds of smaller cascades. You'll spend the night at the Glen Aulin High Sierra Camp, at the foot of the White Cascade. On the second day you'll keep following the Tuolumne downstream for another 3.8 miles and you'll see the California, LeConte and Waterwheel falls. You'll spend another night at the High Sierra Camp and on the third day follow the Tuolumne back to Tuolumne Meadows. On your way to and from Glen Aulin you'll also enjoy views of the Cathedral Range and the Sierra Crest.

Like all the High Sierra Camps, Glen Aulin requires reservations months in advance. However, reservations are often cancelled. So if you arrive in Yosemite without reservations, call the High Sierra Desk at 209-454-2002 and inquire about cancellations. You might get one. For more information on the High Sierra Camps, see pages 26-28.

To reach the trailhead for this Walk, turn onto a paved road that begins on the north side of the Tioga Road, about a mile east of the Tuolumne Meadows Visitor Center and just a few yards east of the bridge over the Tuolumne River. The turnoff is marked by signs saying, among other things, "Glen Aulin," "Soda Springs" and "Stables." Follow the paved road to the left. The trailhead is about .3 miles ahead, at a gate where the road turns sharply to the right and goes uphill to the stables. Park along the road after the turn, walk around the gate and start following the wide trail across the flat meadow toward the Soda Springs and Glen Aulin.

Signs along the way explain that this part of the trail is the remains of the original Tioga Road, which was built in 1883 to service the Great Sierra Mine near Tioga Pass (see Walk No. 24). Other signs describe the trees, animals, scenery and natural history of Tuolumne Meadows (Walk No. 20). One sign points out that the meadow was once covered by a 2,000-foot-deep glacier. Another describes the subtly different habitats of the evergreens growing on the edges of the meadow — how the double-needle lodgepole pines flourish in wetter areas, how Sierra Junipers like sunny, south-facing slopes and how hemlocks prefer shadier, north-facing hillsides.

You'll also have views of the landmarks of Tuolumne Meadows. Behind you is Lembert Dome (Walk No. 21), which rises almost 900 feet above the meadow. On your left, south of the meadow, are, from left to right, the sharp points of Unicorn and Cathedral peaks, flecked with snow even in July, and the rounded gray rock of Fairview Dome.

About .4 miles from the trailhead, the road di-

LeConte Falls slides down ledges and crashes into rocks on the Tuolumne River, west of the **Glen Aulin High Sierra Camp** *(Walk No. 26).* ▶

vides. The left fork goes to a bridge over the Tuolumne (Walk No. 20). Take the right fork, which goes up a grassy slope, to the right of the Soda Springs (described in Walk No. 20). In less than 500 feet you'll come to a trail that leaves the road on the right. A steel sign beside the path says that Glen Aulin High Sierra Camp is 4.7 miles ahead.

Follow the trail, which winds through a rocky, sunny forest of scrub lodgepole pines. You'll soon see a marsh through the trees on your left.

After about .5 miles the path starts to descend gradually and the woods become denser. After about three-quarters of a mile you'll come to an unsigned trail junction. The trail on the right goes to the stables and is used mainly by pack trains. Keep going straight ahead.

Immediately after the trail junction you'll cross a branch of Delaney Creek on stones. Look downstream and you can see the creek flowing prettily over ledge. Immediately after the crossing you'll come to a larger branch of the creek. You may have to walk upstream a few yards to find a place to cross without getting your feet wet.

The woods become more open now and you can see Unicorn and Cathedral peaks through the trees on your left. About .2 miles after your second crossing of Delaney Creek you come to a third and much smaller branch of the stream, which you cross easily on stones. Now you have even better views of Cathedral and Unicorn peaks and, from left to right, of Fairview, Daff and Pothole domes.

Now the trail briefly follows a tiny stream on the left and, about two miles from the trailhead, brings you to another junction. The trail on the right goes to the Young Lakes; Glen Aulin is straight ahead.

You'll immediately cross the stream on your left and walk across a ledgy slope. Fairview Dome and Cathedral and Unicorn peaks again appear on your left.

Then you'll walk down a wide, open ledge, where the trail is marked by cairns, and you'll have another view of Daff and Fairview domes. (If you lose the trail on the ledge, don't worry: you'll see it again at the bottom of the ledge, on your right.)

The trail then runs through shady woods, past a 100-foot-high gray rock outcrop on the right, and gently descends to a flat meadow along the Tuolumne River.

From this grassy floodplain you can see Unicorn and Cathedral peaks and the Cockscomb between them. From here they look so sharp that, if you could run your hand across them, they would cut it. You can also see Pothole Dome, now just three-quarters of a mile away, and Daff Dome, which is more than 300 feet taller than Pothole and just to the right of it.

The trail quickly reaches the banks of the Tuolumne — here as wide as a pond — and immediately crosses a pretty branch of Dingley Creek. The stream is 15 feet wide but only a few inches deep as it flows softly into the river, and its bed is thickly and elegantly cobbled with thousands of different-colored stones that glisten and sparkle in the clear, lapping water. You're now about halfway to the High Sierra Camp. If you feel like taking a break, this is a fine place to do it. (If you want to cross the

creek without getting your feet wet you may have to ford it a few yards upstream from the path.)

The trail next crosses two much smaller branches of Dingley Creek, then crosses another streamlet as it curves along the lodgepole-shaded banks of the Tuolumne.

The trail then moves away from the river and runs over stone causeways (raised paths bordered and supported by stones) as it passes through a small meadow.

Then the path crosses an enormous, smooth, gray-white ledge that rises hundreds of feet above the river, on your right, and slopes elegantly into and under the river like a vast stone beach. Here the Tuolumne is as neat as a water garden. The river flows over its smooth rock bed, then narrows to just 20 feet wide, creating picturesque rapids before flowing transparently over more ledge into a wide stone pool.

The trail goes into the woods again and emerges onto another beachlike ledge which is part of another rock-and-water composition that's even larger than the first one. The river falls in cascades that stretch all the way across its ledge bed, then glides transparently over the ledge in wide, thin sheets before pouring into large rock pools. Look into the smaller pools in the ledge beside the river and you may see tadpoles swimming. Like the first ledge

Vogelsang Lake, on the trail between **Vogelsang High Sierra Camp** *(Walk No. 28) and Vogelsang Pass. Johnson Peak is on the left, the slope of Fletcher Peak on the right.*
◄

"beach," this is one of the Sierra's most charming moving-water features.

The trail goes briefly into the woods yet again before it emerges on more ledge, high above the river. To your left, in the light gray granite on the other side of the river, is the Little Devils Postpile, so-called because its dark gray basalt looks like rows of posts stuck into the earth. It's a smaller version of *the* Devils Postpile, the national monument near Mammoth Lakes. Walk (carefully) out onto the ledge and you'll see the Tuolumne cascading through a deep gorge below you. Look downstream and you'll see the footbridge on which you'll soon cross the river. Farther downstream is Glen Aulin, at the eastern end of the Grand Canyon of the Tuolumne. Rising to the left of the canyon is Falls Ridge. On the right of the canyon is 9,455-foot Wildcat Point.

The trail next runs along the edge of a granite outcrop on your right. Then it switches back and forth on stone ramps to the bottom of the gorge, where the trail is again a soft level path through tall, shady evergreens.

Soon you'll come out of the woods and, about a mile from the High Sierra Camp, you'll cross the sturdy wooden bridge over the Tuolumne. Under the bridge and upstream from it the river is calm. Just below the bridge, however, the Tuolumne abruptly starts its turbulent descent to Glen Aulin.

From here to the High Sierra Camp the trail also descends, often over ledges, stone steps and stone ramps. You'll have occasional views of Mount Conness and other peaks of the Sierra Crest across the river, to the north and northeast. And you'll have even more views of the endlessly cascading Tuolumne, plunging as much as 15 feet over ledges that stretch across the roaring river like dams.

About halfway down to Glen Aulin, the trail leaves the river and reenters the woods, winding through a wet area of corn lilies and sheep laurel before crossing and then following a tiny creek downstream.

Suddenly you'll hear the loudest roar you'll hear all day. Take just a few more steps and you'll see the cluster of large cascades known as Tuolumne Falls. Walk (carefully) out on the ledge beside the falls and get a closer look. The cascades begin when a 14-foot-wide stream of water drops 12 feet and splashes on a ledge. Then the river divides. Some of it leaps down a 40-foot-deep channel into a foaming pool from which mist and rainbows rise. The rest of it trickles, falls and splatters down a 20-foot-high, 40-foot-wide ledge to a deep green pool. Another, ten-foot-wide channel of white water surges beneath your feet and then cascades downstream toward the canyon.

Below the cascades the trail switches back and forth as it descends on stone ramps, past more views of white water. Soon you can glimpse the 40-foot-high falls of the noisily surging White Cascade. Then you'll see the white tents of the High Sierra Camp below the cataract.

About .2 miles from the High Sierra Camp the trail forks. The path on the left goes to May Lake (Walk No. 19). Take the trail on the right, which switches back and forth over stone paving as it descends to the river. Cross the Tuolumne on the steel bridge and look to your right for a vista of both the White Cascade and the top of Tuolumne Falls directly above it.

The White Cascade begins when the Tuolumne surges through a notch at the top of a 70-foot-high ledge that stretches across the river. The torrent crashes into a knob on the ledge and splits into three falls, the largest of which is a thick column of white water that plunges 35 feet into the lake-size pool at the base of the cascades. Another fall drops about 30 feet into the pool and the third falls 12 feet to splatter on a ledge, where it divides again. Part of the third cascade drops 20 feet, directly into the pool; the rest slides down the ledge into the water. Still other, much smaller cascades flow out of the ledge to the left of the major falls.

After crossing the Tuolumne, the trail follows Conness Creek upstream for about 100 feet, then crosses the creek on a large wooden footbridge on your right.

Now you're on the sandy, evergreen-shaded grounds of the High Sierra Camp. The office/dining room/store tent is to your left. The guest tents are on your right, just a few feet from the 150-foot-wide pool at the base of the White Cascade.

* * *

The next day you can take the 7.6-mile round trip down the Tuolumne for a look at six major falls. This Walk is relatively long and relatively demanding. You climb about 1,000 feet and the open ledges along the river can get warm in the summer. Plus there's a lot to see. So give yourself as much time as possible by beginning the Walk immediately after breakfast.

To get to the trail, recross Conness Creek and go right. In about 30 feet you'll see the trail to Waterwheel Falls on your left. You'll immediately climb over a small ridge and you'll see the Tuolumne cascading down the steep canyon on your left. Look behind you and you'll see the White Cascade and Tuolumne Falls above it.

The trail now switches back and forth down the ridge, beside the noisy white river. Then it runs along the bottom of a large, smooth granite ledge that slopes up to the right, high above the trail.

Next the path enters shady woods beside the river. On your left, foaming cascades rush into a long stretch of flat water. For the next mile or so an unusually smooth and level trail follows an unusually smooth and quiet river, utterly unlike the steep, surging, cascading torrent above and below the High Sierra Camp. Through the trees you can also glimpse the steep, bare walls of the canyon.

The trail soon crosses another smooth ledge that runs, uninterrupted, from the edge of the river, on your left, to the top of the steep slope on your right.

Then the trail goes away from the river, switches back and forth down an open, sunny area and crosses a small stream on stones.

Next the trail returns to the Tuolumne, crosses another tiny creek on stones and goes across another ledge that sweeps upward from the river.

Now the path heads toward a high, rocky knob — a shoulder of 9,455-foot Wildcat Point — and skirts its rough talus base as it passes through a wet area thick with corn lilies and ferns. Here you start hearing the sound of falling water—faintly at first, then louder.

Suddenly the trail comes to a deep green pool in the Tuolumne. Just ahead, downstream, the river pours over a flat ledge to begin the .2-mile stretch of cascades known as the California Falls. Now the trail emerges onto bare, sunny, stony ledges and switches back and forth, over rock steps and ramps, next to the falling river. All around you are the steep, almost bare rock walls of the canyon. On your right is the near-vertical rock slope of Wildcat Point. From the wide, bare ledges on the left side of the trail you can see some of the most exciting waterfalls in the park. Many of these ledges have been polished smooth by glaciers so they're slippery, especially when wet. Walk on them carefully.

The first fall, about 40 feet wide, drops 15 feet and then slides almost 100 feet down a ledge, spreading from about 30 feet to about 50 feet wide before crashing into another ledge. Beside it, another fall, about 12 feet wide, spills nearly six feet over a ledge, splatters on the rock and slides transparently down an ochre ledge before joining the flow from the first fall.

Further downstream is another fall, about 40 feet wide and 30 feet high and surrounded on all sides by bare rock. It drops in a neat, all-white parallelogram and looks almost manmade.

The third fall is perhaps the most beautiful on the Walk. It's a pure white ribbon of water that flows in a large, elegant reverse S-curve at the bottom of a

70-foot-long, ochre-colored flume. The white cascade plunges into a green pool and the column of water bubbling underwater looks like a creme de menthe parfait.

The last fall is a 50-foot-long, 20-foot-wide mass of frothing white water that plunges into a handsome rock bound pool, as deep and as wide as a small swimming pool.

The river calms down again but, after just a few hundred feet, plunges through gaps in a damlike ledge and, for the next third of a mile or so, makes a wild descent through ledge sluiceways and over and around boulders and ledges in hundreds of small cascades. The trail also descends, over a rough, sunny talus slope, past wildflowers and chinquapin and manzanita bushes, and beneath the almost vertical walls of the canyon on your right.

Finally, you reach a sign that says you're 3.3 miles from Glen Aulin. On your left, beyond a few tree-shaded campsites, is LeConte Falls. The cascades are broad, thin sheets of water — some of them as much as 30 feet wide — that flow hundreds of feet down the wide, steeply sloping ledge that stretches across the river. The cascades rush down the ledge so fast that when they run into bumps on the rock they bounce into the air and then drop back onto the ledge in a small waterfall. LeConte is an excellent spot for a rest or picnic. Just stretch out beside your favorite bit of rushing water and enjoy the show.

After LeConte Falls, the trail switches back and forth through open sun-washed ledges as it continues to follow the river downstream. However, you'll still see the falls on your left.

Then the trail becomes more level as it goes away from the river, past manzanita and chinquapin, and runs briefly through evergreens. Through the trees on your left you'll see green pools in the river.

About .5 miles from LeConte Falls you'll come to the top of Waterwheel Falls, a set of long, narrow cascades that roars down a trough in the ledge to the left of the trail. If the falls are full enough and fast enough, some of the falling water hits the ledge rock with such force and at such an angle that it bounces upward and rolls backward until it makes a complete circle—like a wheel. Remember that true waterwheels roll *backward* and are rare. Don't confuse them with the rather common (though also exciting) phenomenon—seen, for example, at LeConte Falls—of falling water hitting rock and bouncing upward and *forward*.

It's a steep climb down to the bottom of the falls—you descend 400 feet in a quarter-mile—it's an even steeper climb coming back and the round trip will add another half-mile to your Walk, making it a total of 8.1 miles. What's more, nearly all the climbing in the Walk—1,000 feet from the top of Waterwheel Falls to Glen Aulin—remains to be done on your return to the High Sierra Camp. So unless the waterwheels are turning, or unless you've got a lot of extra time and energy, you may want to turn around here. Whatever you do, try to spend as much time as you can at your favorite falls before you have to get back to the camp in time for dinner.

27 Sunrise High Sierra Camp

This moderately strenuous three-day excursion takes you to some of the best views in the park. On the first day you'll walk 5.3 miles from Tenaya Lake to Sunrise High Sierra Camp. En route you'll have continuous views of Mount Hoffmann and Toulumne Peak and you'll pass the pretty Sunrise Lakes. You'll spend the night, and see a panoramic mountain view, at the High Sierra Camp. The next day you'll take the John Muir Trail on a ten-mile round trip to Upper Cathedral Lake. On the way you'll have many intimate views of the Columbia Finger, Tresidder Peak, Matthes Crest, Cathedral and Echo peaks and other summits of the Cathedral and Clark ranges. After a second night at the High Sierra Camp you'll retrace your steps to Tenaya Lake — and this time you'll be walking "into" most of the views.

Like the trail around Tenaya Lake (Walk No. 18), this excursion begins in the parking area on the east side of the Tioga Road near the southwestern end of Tenaya Lake. Follow the route of the Tenaya Lake Walk (page 116) until you come to the junction where the trail along the lake goes to the left and the path to Sunrise High Sierra Camp goes to the right.

After the junction the trail parallels Tenaya Creek for about a quarter-mile. On your right, through the lodgepole pines, you'll have occasional views of the creek — here as still as a lake — and the meadows around it.

Then the trail moves away from the creek, passes through a moist woods and climbs gently through a rocky area to a small, ledgy rise. From here you can see Tenaya Peak and other evergreen-festooned rock sculpture of the Tenaya Lake basin, on your left, and the bare summit of Mount Hoffmann, including its chimney and double ramparts, on your right.

Now the trail descends quickly to the outlet of Mildred Lake. After crossing the creek on rocks, you follow the winding path through an often level and sometimes wet lodgepole forest.

Next you cross several tiny streams on stones and briefly follow a stream on your right, which is an outlet of the Sunrise Lakes. Through the trees you can see a meadow on the other side of the creek. Soon you cross several wide branches of the stream on stones. If you look through the trees on your left here, you may be able to see the creek cascading over ledges.

Now you start climbing the ridge on your left. The last time we were here it had rained heavily for several days and dozens of tiny streamlets were cascading and trickling beautifully down the slopes.

The trail soon emerges on ledges where lilies, asters, Indian paintbrush, lupine and other wild-flowers flourish in the sun. If you look behind you

you'll have a 90-degree view. Mount Hoffman and Tuolumne Peak will be on the left, Tenaya Peak on the right. As you climb higher you'll see, hundreds of feet below, pools and cascades in the silver ribbon of Tenaya Creek as it flows over the bare, gray mile-wide rock trough of Tenaya Canyon. You can also see cars on the Tioga Road above the canyon's west wall. (Use binoculars and you'll get an even better view.)

The views of Mount Hoffmann, Tuolumne Peak and Tenaya Canyon will stay with you as the trail switches back and forth up the canyon's steep upper slope. This part of the trail is among the steepest of any Great Walk in the park—you'll gain 800 feet in only three-quarters of a mile. However, the climbing will be accompanied by some of the best views in the park. So take your time and rest often—your climb will be easier and you'll have more time to appreciate views you will see nowhere else.

About halfway to the High Sierra Camp the trail passes through hemlocks, finally levels off and quickly comes to a junction. The trail on the left goes to the High Sierra Camp, the one on the right to Clouds Rest.

Follow the High Sierra Camp trail through a rocky lodgepole forest and past the steep, bare west slope of 9,974-foot Sunrise Mountain, on your right. You'll also have occasional views, to your rear, of Half Dome and Clouds Rest.

About .3 miles from the junction you'll reach Lower Sunrise Lake, a 300-foot-wide tarn tucked beside the steep, bare rock slope of Sunrise Mountain and surrounded by rocks and scattered evergreen trees. The trail curves around the north shore of the lake, crossing its outlet on stones and logs and passing handsome clumps of heather and Labrador tea.

Then the trail climbs gently past Middle Sunrise Lake, which is about 300 feet to the left of the path and about 50 feet below it. The middle lake is about the same size as the lower one and it's surrounded by forest and dotted with tiny rock islands. Above the tarn you can see Mount Hoffmann.

The trail keeps climbing up open, rocky woods between the ends of two ridges. You'll glimpse Clouds Rest through the trees to your right.

Then the trail climbs along the right side of the creek that cascades from Upper Sunrise Lake to the middle lake. Soon you'll cross the creek and enjoy a wide view: Mount Hoffmann on your left, Tenaya Peak straight ahead, the creek sliding 200 feet down a ledge at your feet, and the middle lake below.

About 3.5 miles from the trailhead the path levels off and you can see Upper Sunrise Lake. The trail now follows the flat, grassy southwestern shore of the 500-foot-long lake, the largest of the three. You'll pass campsites and clumps of heather and Labrador tea as you head toward the steep, bare rock ridge at the lake's eastern end.

Then you climb away from the lake and up a gully. The path will parallel a creek, on your left, flowing into the lake. Soon you'll cross both the creek and the gully, then immediately cross another, smaller inlet and climb up an open forest of hemlock and pine. Turn around often here, both to rest and to enjoy views of the lake and Mount Hoffmann and

Tuolumne Peak beyond it. You'll also have occasional views of Tresidder Peak and the Columbia Finger to your left.

Less than .4 miles from the upper lake the grade eases and you cross an unusually wide, flat, bare sandy pass. At almost 9,800 feet above sea level, this is the highest point of the Walk. In front of you is the snowcapped Clark Range.

Now the path gently descends through open, gravel-floored lodgepole woods. Through the trees you'll have views of a meadow on your right. You'll also catch glimpses of the Clark Range straight ahead and the Echo Peaks, Matthes Crest, Mount Florence and other Sierra Crest peaks on your left.

Then the trail curves sharply to the left. Now the occasional views of mountains and the southern end of Long Meadow will be on your right.

Finally, the trail switches back and forth down a steep slope, past several campsites and several small creeks (which you cross on rocks), until you see the white tents of the High Sierra Camp.

The camp is built on a small grassy shelf just above Long Meadow. From viewpoints nearby you can enjoy a panoramic vista of mountains. From right to left, you can see, in the southeast, the pyramid-shaped summits of the Clark Range, including Mount Clark and Gray, Red, Ottaway, Merced and Triple Divide peaks; Sierra Crest peaks, including Mount Ansel Adams, 12,561-foot Mount Florence, the seventh highest peak in the park, which has snow year round; 12,960-foot Mount Maclure, the park's third highest peak; 13,114-foot Mount Lyell, the highest summit in

Yosemite; and Simmons and Vogelsang peaks. In the foreground, on the opposite side of the meadow, is Bug Dome and, in an arc running from east to north (or right to left) are Rafferty Peak, the Kuna Crest (part of the Sierra Crest) and the sharp-edged, bare rock landmarks of the northern Cathedral Range, including the long fin of Matthes Crest, the many-pointed Echo Peaks, Cathedral Peak and the Eichorn Pinnacle, which is attached to Cathedral Peak like a thumb to a hand; the sharply pointed Columbia Finger and the rectangular Tresidder Peak.

* * *

The moderate, ten-mile round trip to Upper Cathedral Lake (Walk No. 22) also offers close views of the sharp-pointed summits of the northern Cathedral Range, including Matthes Crest, the Echo Peaks, Cathedral Peak and the Eichorn Pinnacle, Tresidder Peak and the Columbia Finger.

The Walk begins beside the camp dining tent. Go down the stone steps beside the cascade and follow the John Muir Trail along the north side of the quarter-mile-wide meadow. You'll walk past large drifts of blooming wildflowers, as well as marmots, Belding ground squirrels and, if you're lucky, deer. The Clark Range and Mount Florence will be on your right. Bug Dome, on the east side of the L-shaped meadow, will be straight ahead and Rafferty Peak will be in the distance, to the left of Bug Dome.

After about a quarter-mile the trail swings to the north and follows the western edge of the meadow. Bug Dome is now on your right, Tresidder Peak, the Columbia Finger and the Echo Peaks are ahead of you and the snowy summit of Mount Florence is behind you.

After crossing several small creeks on stones, the trail enters grassy, open lodgepole pine woods and, almost a mile from the camp, comes to a junction. The path to the right goes to Merced Lake High Sierra Camp. Stay on the John Muir Trail, which goes straight ahead and quickly brings you to a branch of Cathedral Fork, whose bed is lined with pretty rust-colored rocks.

Cross the creek on stones and follow it up through a meadow. Behind you is another view of the Clark Range. Ahead of you is the long, pointed Columbia Finger and, behind it, Tresidder Peak, which from here looks like one wall of a ruined turreted castle.

About two miles from the camp, the trail heads away from the creek and toward the Columbia Finger. Then the path goes into the woods and climbs in earnest, on a rocky trail, up the steep slope to the right of the Columbia Finger.

After less than a quarter-mile, however, the trail gradually levels off, the woods become more open and you begin to enjoy panoramic vistas from ledgy viewpoints along the trail. On the right, in the distance, you see the peaks of the Clark Range and the Sierra Crest. Just a mile or so away are the delicate rock sculptures of the Cathedral Range, including the long fin of the Matthes Crest, ahead, and the Echo Peaks, to the left.

The views get better as the trail climbs almost imperceptibly through open, gravelly woods. On your left, you have another view of the Columbia Finger. From here it looks not like a finger but like a butte with flat, nearly vertical sides. On the other hand, Tresidder Peak, which also appears again on the left, now has a tall finger in the middle of it. Soon Cathedral Peak and the Eichorn Pinnacle also join the panorama and you are all but surrounded by two-mile-high pinnacles that were too high for the glaciers to grind down. Instead, the glaciers enhanced the peaks by wearing away their sides, making them even steeper. Now the almost fragile-looking promontories are a giant garden of delicate, natural granite sculpture.

Gradually the trail descends through the open woods to a meadow. As you get closer to Cathedral Peak you can see the half-dozen tiny spires on its right summit.

The trail then goes over a sandy pass and suddenly you can see Upper Cathedral Lake in the wide meadow below. The path quickly takes you down to its undulating, grassy shores, from which you can enjoy views of Cathedral and Echo peaks and the slopes of Tresidder Peak. (See the next-to-last paragraph of Walk No. 22, Cathedral Lakes, on page 139 for a description of the panorama.) The lake's smooth shoreside ledges are also perfect places to enjoy a leisurely picnic lunch.

When you're ready, follow the path back to the High Sierra Camp and enjoy the views again from another perspective.

28 Vogelsang High Sierra Camp

This moderate three-day round trip takes you closer to more major mountains than any other Great Walk in Yosemite. On the first day you'll take the 6.7-mile walk from Tuolumne Meadows to the Vogelsang High Sierra Camp, at the foot of snow-flecked Fletcher Peak. On your way to (or from) Vogelsang you can take a two-mile round trip to Boothe Lake. You'll spend the night at the camp and the next day take a three-mile round trip to Vogelsang Pass and a two-mile round trip to Evelyn Lake for splendid mountain views. After spending a second night at the camp you'll retrace your steps to Tuolumne Meadows.

If you can take only one or two of the three side trips at Vogelsang, note that we rank Vogelsang Pass as the best Walk and Evelyn Lake second best. (See the descriptions below.)

You can begin this Walk at one of two trailheads near the Tuolumne Meadows Lodge. To reach either one, take the paved road to the lodge, which begins on the south side of the Tioga Road, about 1.5 miles east of the Tuolumne Meadows Visitor Center. About .4 miles from the Tioga Road you'll come to the first trailhead: the hikers' parking area on the left (which is also the beginning of Walk No. 21, to Lembert Dome and Dog Lake). The trail begins on the right side of the road and follows the Dana Fork of the Tuolumne River upstream until, in about a quarter-mile, it comes to a wooden footbridge over the river. The second trailhead is at the southwest corner of the Tuolumne Lodge parking lot, which is about .3 miles beyond the first trailhead. The trail goes south through the woods until, about 100 feet from the parking lot, it reaches both the footbridge over the Dana Fork and the path from the first trailhead.

Cross the bridge over the rocky-bottomed fork and follow the John Muir Trail upstream. In a couple of hundred feet the trail forks. Go right and follow the wide, smooth, sandy path through a forest of small lodgepole pines. You'll pass a little meadow on your left, then start descending to the Lyell Fork of the Tuolumne River.

You'll quickly emerge onto a large, flat meadow and you'll have views, through the trees, of Cathedral and Unicorn peaks on your right and Mammoth Peak to your left. You'll also start hearing the Lyell Fork.

About .5 miles from the Dana Fork you'll reach the footbridge over the Lyell Fork, which is a destination in itself. Beneath the handsome wooden bridge the stream flows transparently over wide, smooth ledges. Upstream the creek is the focal point of a lovely pastoral composition. The wide river gleams in the sun as it flows serenely through the long, wide, evergreen-bordered meadow. The bare, pointed massif of Mammoth Peak rises in the distance.

As you cross the creek, notice the three-foot-wide pothole on your right, in the ledge between the two spans of the bridge. And when you reach the southern end of the bridge, take another look upstream. You'll see Mount Gibbs, to the left of Mammoth, and Mount Dana, to the left of Gibbs.

Walk another couple of hundred feet and the trail forks again. Go left and follow the nearly level path through a sun-dappled forest. Through the trees on your left you'll have views of the meadow you just crossed. In about another .5 miles you'll cross a small clearing, across which you'll have a view of Lembert Dome (Walk No. 21) to your rear.

About a mile from the trailhead, just before a footbridge over Rafferty Creek, you'll reach another trail junction. Take the path to the right, which almost immediately starts switching back and forth up a stony slope. Although the path will follow Rafferty Creek for the next four miles, views of the stream will be rare, especially at first. On the other hand, as you climb the steep slope, you'll have better and better views of Tuolumne Meadows, behind you, and, from left to right, Mount Dana, Mount Gibbs and Mammoth Peak, all on your left. If you take your time here and rest often at the viewpoints, your climb will be easier and you'll have more time to savor the scenery.

Happily, the stiff climb lasts only a quarter-mile or so. Then the trail nearly levels off and climbs only gradually, almost imperceptibly, through an increasingly open rocky and ledgy evergreen forest.

On your right will be the steep, bare rock slopes of the six-mile-long, two-mile-high ridge that parallels Rafferty Creek. You'll also have occasional views of 11,408-foot Fletcher Peak and 11,516-foot Vogelsang Peak, ahead, and the snow-topped peaks of the Sierra Crest, on the northeast boundary of the park, to your rear.

After crossing several tiny tributaries of Rafferty Creek, the trail will come within half a mile of a steep, gray rock shoulder of 11,070-foot Johnson Peak, on your right. You're now about halfway to the High Sierra Camp and Rafferty Creek is just a few yards to the left of the trail. The creek's grassy banks and almost still pools are a pleasant place for a picnic.

The trail now runs into deeper woods and then curves to the right of a wet, grassy meadow, which is bisected by the meandering Rafferty Creek. Notice the rectangular orange-and-black California Cooperative Snow Survey markers nailed to some of the trees.

After crossing some more trickling tributaries of the creek, the path again climbs steeply but briefly and you'll have more views of peaks to your rear.

Then the trail starts to climb gently along the right side of a rolling, rocky, mile-long meadow. Ridges rise on your left and right and you have constant views of Sierra Crest peaks behind you and of jagged, snowy Fletcher and Vogelsang peaks, now just a couple of miles ahead.

The meadow gets wider and the views get better as you gradually ascend to Tuolumne Pass. You'll cross many meandering tributaries of Rafferty

Creek as the trail crosses the meadow and, almost six miles from the trailhead, reaches Tuolumne Pass. The pass, almost two miles high, is marked by a pair of tiny tarns surrounded by grass and rocks. One pond drains toward the north slope of the pass, into Rafferty Creek and then the Tuolumne River. The other pond drains toward the south slope, into Emeric Creek, Emeric Lake, Fletcher Creek and the Merced River.

Just south of the tarns the trail divides. The left fork goes to the High Sierra Camp. The right fork goes to Boothe Lake and four tiny ponds beyond it. (If you don't feel like taking this two-mile side trip now, go directly to the High Sierra Camp.)

* * *

The Boothe Lake trail gradually descends from the pass and brings you within sight of Boothe Lake, on your right, in about .3 miles. The quarter-mile-long lake is bordered by meadows on its south, east and west shores and by evergreen-dappled crags rising steeply above its north shore. You'll pass several trails, on the right, that go down to the east shore of the lake.

In about .5 miles the trail reaches the west shore of the lake, where you have a close view of the 11,200-foot-high Choochoo, a rock outcrop on top of the ridge above the lake that looks like the silhouette of a toy railroad train. To the southeast, you'll see the top of Fletcher Peak.

The trail now follows a long, narrowing meadow away from the lake and quickly brings you to a 50-foot-wide, 300-foot-long pond encircled by grass. Then the path briefly follows a streamlet through another narrow meadow and soon brings you to the largest pond in the chain: a 200-foot-wide, 300-foot-long lakelet bordered by ledges and grass. It even has a tiny island with a thick growth of pine trees. On the opposite side of the trail is another grass-ringed pond, equally long but only 50 to 100 feet wide. Immediately beyond the second and third ponds is a much smaller one, in a tiny, sunny meadow. The trail parallels the undulating borders of the four ponds and, at the same time, offers views of Fletcher and Vogelsang peaks.

* * *

After you've enjoyed these charming woodland pools, turn around, follow the path back to the trail junction at Tuolumne Pass and take the trail to the High Sierra Camp, which gradually climbs the northern slope of Fletcher Peak. On your right you'll see the Choochoo and, to the right of the Choochoo, 11,110-foot Rafferty Peak. You'll also see Boothe Lake and, to your rear, the peaks of the Sierra Crest.

In about .6 miles the trail switches back to the left and quickly climbs to a meadow that has one of the most exciting mountain views in the park. Directly ahead is Fletcher Peak, steep, bare and snowflecked even in July. On your right is Vogelsang Peak, taller and even more massive than Fletcher.

You'll pass signs indicating that campsites and toilets are to the left. Keep following the path straight ahead and you'll quickly come to a trail junction just a few yards from the High Sierra Camp.

At 10,180 feet, Vogelsang is both the highest High Sierra Camp and one of the best located: at the base of Fletcher Peak, on the ledgy banks of briskly flowing Fletcher Creek and just a couple of hundred feet from Fletcher Lake. The camp also has clear views of the Choochoo and Rafferty Peak to the west and Ragged Peak, Sheep Peak, White Mountain, Mount Conness and other Sierra Crest peaks to the north.

* * *

The moderate three-mile round trip to 10,720-foot Vogelsang Pass will reward you with views of five mountain lakes, the "back" of Half Dome and Clouds Rest, and a stirring panorama of some of the highest peaks in the park.

The Walk begins on the ledges on the west side of the camp dining tent. The trail, marked by a row of stones on each side of the path, descends to a wide pool in Fletcher Creek. Turn left and walk about 50 feet upstream, where you cross the creek—here pouring through a chute in the ledge—on a pair of logs. You'll cross three smaller streams on stones as you traverse a wet meadow and then start a moderate climb of the western slope of Fletcher Peak.

Views will quickly appear: the Sierra Crest to your rear; the Choochoo and Rafferty and Johnson peaks to your right rear; Emeric Lake, surrounded by bare rock, in the valley to your right; and the smaller Babcock Lake to the left of Emeric. Ahead of you, the twin towers of Vogelsang Peak and the long saddle between them make the top of the massif look like the silhouette of a suspension bridge.

After only about .2 miles the trail levels off. You can't see the lakes anymore but, just to the right of Vogelsang, you can glimpse a rare view of the eastern or "back" sides of both Half Dome and, to the right of Half Dome, Clouds Rest. Notice the distinctive overhang or "diving board" on the top right-hand side of Half Dome. Here, too, you get your first look at the grassy shores of Vogelsang Lake, which lies in the bottom of a vast, steep rock bowl formed by the smooth wall of Fletcher Peak on the left, the much rougher slopes of Vogelsang Peak on the right and the steep slope of Vogelsang Pass straight ahead. You can also see the top of 12,561-foot Mount Florence peeking above the pass.

You quickly descend to the quarter-mile-long lake and cross its outlet on carefully placed trunks of trees.

The path then heads to the right, along the western shore of the lake, then climbs across a rocky meadow above the lake, following a small creek.

The trail crosses the creek, then runs through double rows of stones as it traverses ledge. You now have constant views, to your left rear, of the Sierra Crest. Also on your left is the lake and a long boulder-island offshore that looks like a narwhal.

Soon you cross another small creek and, behind you, catch a glimpse of the tents of the High Sierra Camp.

Then the trail goes off the ledge and climbs the sandy treeless slopes of Vogelsang Pass, southeast of the lake. You can't see the Sierra Crest or the High Sierra Camp anymore but you can still see the Choochoo and Rafferty Peak.

Soon you cross yet another creek, tumbling over rocks in tiny cascades. Then the path switches back and forth and you see Mount Florence again, on the other side of the pass. Suddenly you're at the top of the pass, which is marked by a minute, 50-foot-wide pond surrounded by pinkish granite rocks.

You quickly cross to the north side of the narrow pass and there it is—one of the most spectacular vistas in the High Sierra! For your best view go just a few yards more, to where the trail starts its long descent to Lewis Creek. The mountain panorama before you, from Fletcher Peak on the left to Vogelsang on the right, includes 12,080-foot Parsons Peak; 12,503-foot Simmons Peak; 12,960-foot Mount Maclure, the third highest summit in Yosemite; the wide massif of 12,561-foot Mount Florence, the park's seventh highest peak, straight ahead—all less than four miles away—then, about eight miles away, the summits of the Clark Range: Triple Divide and Merced peaks, Red and Gray peaks (both named, with rough accuracy, for their colors), Mount Clark and the cliff in front of Mount Clark known as the Obelisk. Below you, in the meadow on your left, is blue Gallison Lake and, to the right of it, the long cascading ribbon of its outlet. The larger, blue-green Bernice Lake is at the base of Mount Florence. Both of these lakes drain into Lewis Creek, which meanders through the meadow 1,000 feet below you. Just a portion of this panorama—just the summits from Fletcher Peak to Mount Florence, for example—would have been magnificent. But this relatively close view of so many mountains from just one place makes the vista the rival of Glacier Point.

Needless to say, this incomparable place is perfect for a picnic or at least a very long pause. When you're ready, follow the path back to the High Sierra Camp and walk "into" the views of Vogelsang Lake and the mountains beyond it.

* * *

The undemanding two-mile round trip to Evelyn Lake offers often-continuous mountain views, including an 180-degree panorama of the Sierra Crest.

The Walk begins at the trail junction just north of the High Sierra Camp. Follow the roadlike, double-rutted path that runs northeast across the wide meadow about 200 feet from Fletcher Lake. You'll have views all around you: Fletcher and Vogelsang peaks to your right, the Choochoo to your left and the Sierra Crest ahead.

The views continue as the trail climbs gently through pine trees on a sunny slope for about .7 miles. After leveling off briefly the trail climbs again. Finally it passes through a small, grassy ravine and gains the top of a small rise.

Suddenly you'll see a flat, mile-wide meadow dotted with tiny lakes and ringed by mountains. On the right side of the meadow, at the foot of a steep, bare slope, is the elliptical, .4-mile-long Evelyn Lake. Beyond the meadow is a 180-degree mountain panorama that stretches from the Choochoo and Rafferty and Johnson peaks on the left, to the Sierra Crest a dozen miles to the north, to 11,932-foot Amelia Earhart Peak on the right.

After you've savored one of the widest, longest mountain views in the Sierras, turn around and follow the path back to the High Sierra Camp.

Notice

Every effort has been made to ensure the accuracy of all information in this guide. Nevertheless, due to human and natural factors beyond the control of this guide, no Walk in Yosemite is absolutely risk free. Great Walks Inc. can therefore assume no liability for any accidents or injuries incurred while taking these Walks.

Great Walks of Sequoia & Kings Canyon National Parks

Sequoia & Kings Canyon National Parks are just a few hours' drive from Yosemite and the twin parks have a total of 42 Great Walks—more than almost any other national park.

Eleven Walks take you into dense groves of giant sequoias, the world's largest living things. Six Walks bring you to waterfalls. Four feature pictographs and other Indian artifacts. Two Walks include tours of limestone caves. Four take you over lovely oak- and grass-covered foothills. And more than half the Walks offer wide views of mountains and water- and glacier-carved canyons that are among the deepest in the world.

All 42 Walks are carefully described in *Great Walks of Sequoia & Kings Canyon National Parks*. Like all Great Walks guides, *Sequoia & Kings Canyon* is pocket size and lavishly illustrated with beautiful, full-color photographs.

To order your copy send $8.95 plus $1.50 for shipping and handling to: Great Walks, PO Box 410, Goffstown, NH 03045. Your guide will be sent to you immediately.

Like Yosemite, Sequoia and Kings Canyon National Parks are located along the two-mile-high crest of the Sierra Nevada. If you like Yosemite you'll also enjoy Sequoia and Kings Canyon. And no guide will help you enjoy it more than *Great Walks of Sequoia & Kings Canyon*. Order your copy now!

Other Great Walks guides already published:

►*Great Walks of Acadia National Park & Mount Desert Island:* 29 Great Walks and three Honorable Mentions on Maine's Mount Desert Island, known for its low, ledge-topped mountains, forest-ringed lakes and rockbound, island-dotted seacoast;

►*Great Walks of Southern Arizona:* six Walks in the fascinating mountains, canyons and basins of the Sonoran Desert near Phoenix and Tucson;

►*Great Walks of Big Bend National Park:* six Walks in the Chisos Mountains, the deep and narrow canyons of the Rio Grande and the fascinating Chihuahuan Desert at the "big bend" of the Rio Grande in southwest Texas.

►*Great Walks of the Great Smokies:* 20 Walks to historic sites, impressive waterfalls and cascades and exciting mountain vistas in Great Smoky Mountains National Park, which straddles the Appalachian Crest in Tennessee and North Carolina.

►*Great Walks of Sequoia & Kings Canyon National Parks:* 42 Walks with views of deep canyons, evergreen forests, snowcapped mountain peaks and giant sequoia trees—the world's largest living things—in two adjacent parks in California's Sierra Nevada.

The *Sequoia & Kings Canyon* and *Acadia* guides are $8.95 each; the *Great Smokies* guide is $5.95; the *Southern Arizona* and *Big Bend* guides are $3.95 each.

You can buy Great Walks guides in bookstores or order them directly from the publisher by sending a check or money order for the price of each guide you want, plus $1.50 for mailing and handling the order, to: Great Walks, Box 410, Goffstown, NH 03045.

You can also receive more information on the series by sending $1 (deductible from your first order) to Great Walks at the address above.

Own an Original Oktavec Photograph

You can own an original print of any Eileen Oktavec photograph in this guide.

At your request we will custom make a high-quality, 9¼-by-14-inch color print of your favorite Yosemite photograph(s) by Eileen Oktavec. The print(s) will be hand labeled, numbered and signed by the photographer.

An original Oktavec photographic print is many things: a treasured memento of Yosemite, a masterful depiction of its world-famous scenery, a valuable addition to your art collection and, of course, an excellent gift.

To order, simply tell us which print(s) you would like and enclose a check for $86 for each one, plus $4 for shipping and handling the order. Send your order to: Great Walks, PO Box 410, Goffstown, NH 03045. Allow 2-3 weeks for delivery.

About the Author
and Photographer

Robert Gillmore and Eileen Oktavec have been taking Great Walks throughout the United States and Europe for years. A landscape designer, author and publisher, Gillmore was graduated cum laude from Williams College and has a Ph.D. from the University of Virginia. His most recent book is *The Woodland Garden.* Oktavec is a prize-winning artist, photographer, cultural anthropologist and author of *Answered Prayers: Miracles and Milagros Along the Border.* She was graduated from the State University of New York at Stony Brook and has a masters degree from the University of Arizona. Gillmore and Oktavec live in Goffstown, New Hampshire.

To Our Readers:

Please help us stay current. If you discover that anything described in this guide has changed, please let us know so we can make corrections in future editions. Please write to: Great Walks, PO Box 410, Goffstown, NH 03045. Thank you.